THE HISTORY OF
WINCHESTER FIREARMS
DEAN K. BOORMAN

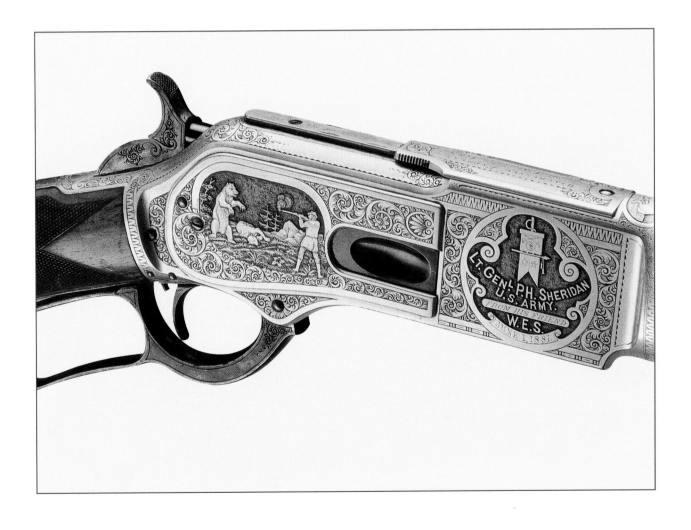

THE HISTORY OF
WINCHESTER FIREARMS

DEAN K. BOORMAN

THE LYONS PRESS

The Author

DEAN K. BOORMAN is President of the prestigious Armor and Arms Club of New York. He is a member of the American Society of Arms Collectors and of the Visiting Committee, Department of Arms and Armor, The Metropolitan Museum of Art, as well as a noted historian on antique and modern firearms. He resides in New York City. He has also written a companion volume to this book, *The History of Colt Firearms.*

Credits

Project Manager: Ray Bonds
Designers: InterPrep Ltd
Picture research: Anne Lang
Color reproduction: Digital Imaging
Printed and bound in Italy

Acknowledgments

The publishers wish to acknowledge the assistance given by U.S. Repeating Arms Co., and Winchester Ammunition, Winchester Division, Olin Corporation, in the preparation of this book, in particular for the reproduction of the "Horse & Rider" logo. (WINCHESTER is a trademark of Olin Corporation and is used by permission. Neither the author nor the publisher are sponsored by or associated with Olin.) Thanks are also due to Philip Schreier of the National Firearms Museum of the National Rifle Association, and to the NRA, for assistance and for supplying several photographs used in this book, as did Winchester Mystery House, Butterfield and Butterfield auctioneers, the Kansas State Historical Society, and the Buffalo Bill Historical Center. The publishers are especially grateful to R. L. Wilson and to G. Allan Brown for permission to reproduce photographs from the book *Winchester: An American Legend.*

Contents

Picture Credits

From *Winchester: An American Legend*,
by R. L. Wilson: page 1, 28 (bottom), 29, 38, 42, 48, 61 (top), 65, 67 (top), 69 (bottom right), 76, 77 (bottom), 78, 80, 84-85, 90, 91 (bottom three), 94. 95, 98 (bottom), 99 (bottom), 101 (bottom, 102, 103, 104, 105, 107, 107, 109, 110 (center), 111 (center right), 113 (bottom right), 115 (bottom), 120 (bottom), 121 (bottom), 123 (bottom).
From Butterfield and Butterfield:
9 (top), 10-11 (bottom), 20, 36-37 (center), 43, 46-47 (above center), 49, 58-59 (bottom three), 64, 66-67 (bottom), 69 (top two), 110-111 (top two and bottom), 112-113 (except bottom right), 114-115 (except third from top, and bottom), 116-117 (except for third from top, left, and bottom), 118-119, 120-121 (center), 122-123 (except bottom right).
From Kansas State Historical Society:
10 (top).

From National Rifle Association:
4-5, 70, 72 (left), 74-75 (bottom two), 120-121 (top two).
From Winchester:
11 (top), 87, 88-89, 92-93, 96-97, 98-99 (except bottom right), 100, 101 (top).
From Buffalo Bill Historical Center:
18-19, 30 (top), 52 (top), 53 (top two).
From Winchester Mystery House:
50, 108 (bottom).
Unless stated above, or with captions, the photographs in this book have been drawn from the archives of Salamander Books. The publishers are grateful for the assistance given by the Buffalo Bill Historical Center and the Gene Autry Western Heritage Museum, where many of the firearms were photographed.

PREFACE

by R. L. Wilson

It has often been said that companies like Winchester and Colt – the "blue chips" of gun collecting – need not advertise or actively promote their products. Both makers have ample amounts of free press through television and the movies, fiction and non-fiction books, articles, and short stories, as well as the world of gun shows, museum exhibits, the rapidly expanding world of re-enactors – and word of mouth.

In the case of Winchester, every time the James Stewart film "Winchester '73" appears on television, the company receives untold value in free publicity. No make of American longarm, the world over, has greater brand recognition that Winchester. In fact, when hearing the company name, one automatically thinks also of "The Gun That Won the West."

Kids from my generation grew up watching Saturday matinee Westerns, in which the standard arms were Winchester rifles and Colt handguns. When "Winchester '73" was released in 1950, Universal-International and the Winchester company launched a masterful publicity campaign, a significant aspect of which was a search for examples of the "1 of 100" and "1 of 1000" rifles, in the Models of 1873 and 1876.

For the first time, a hit Hollywood film had been named after a gun! Such entertainment fueled the imaginations, and the passions, of collectors like myself, and was a crucial element in creating the world of gun collecting as we know it today.

Winchesters offer the collector everything one could wish for in a firearm: art and craftsmanship, history, mechanics, performance, and romance. I will never forget being in the

presence of movie heroes Gene Autry and Monte Hale and their wives as they contemplated purchasing for the Autry Museum a de luxe Winchester Model 1876 rifle custom-made for Theodore Roosevelt. It was Monte who gripped this historic piece and solemnly said, "Just imagine the history and adventure this beautiful Winchester experienced in the hands of one of the greatest Americans who ever lived." That evening decades ago, the museum added this great American treasure to its collections.

The Winchester represents so much of what we Americans cherish, and honor and respect: freedom, our extraordinary industrial, cultural and artistic heritage, the thrill of the hunt, and the romance of the Wild West.

Dean Boorman captures all of that in this handsome new book. And, as the great nephew of pioneer arms and armor expert Dr. Bashford Dean, he has a particular affinity for the role of firearms in the past, present, and future – as well as for the unique position of the Winchester in that saga. Dr. Dean was the founder of the Department of Arms and Armor of The Metropolitan Museum of Art, and thus Dean Boorman

carries on a family tradition begun by that groundbreaking arms expert, whose stature was in the same league as that of Oliver Winchester.

Further, as president of the Armor and Arms Club of New York, Dean Boorman reflects the quite international awareness and appreciation of firearms shared by the membership in that organization – the oldest of its kind in the Western hemisphere (established 1921).

Winchester Firearms will find a ready audience of anyone who appreciates the special roles of firearms, and of entrepreneurs like Oliver Winchester, in America's uniquely fascinating history. I have enjoyed greatly reading this fine work, and take pleasure in recommending it as a title well worthy of a special place in the study and celebration of the legend that is Winchester.

Below: The most famous early Winchester, the Model 1873, showing cocking action of lever, with original cartridges and spent shells. One of the few movies named for a gun was "Winchester '73!"

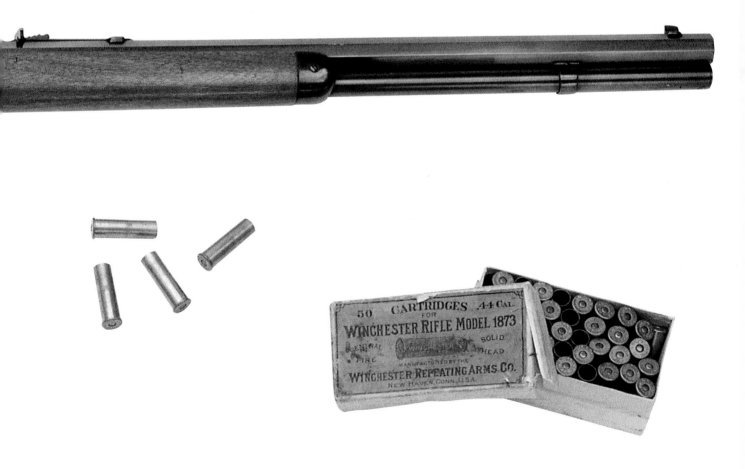

INTRODUCTION

The name "Winchester," like the name "Colt," immediately evokes an image of a famous firearm. Models from both companies have claims to the title "The Gun That Won the West," and products from both represent high quality modern arms which are still used in shooting sports today.

What accounts for this mystique? What makes a "Famous Gun?" To this writer, there are three ingredients that go to make up the formula for fame, all of which apply to Winchester: a major role in history; mechanical innovation combined with esthetic appeal; and company success over an extended period of years. Proof of how well Winchester meets these qualifications is the collector appeal and high prices realized for these arms as antiques and custom models.

Historically, Winchester is best known for the lever action rifle carried in the saddle scabbard of every cowboy movie hero. There is also a general awareness that some of the Native Americans at the Custer massacre at the Little Bighorn in June, 1876, were equipped with Winchester repeaters, while the Seventh Cavalry troopers had to defend themselves with single-shot Springfield carbines. However, less well known is that Oliver Winchester started his company as early as the beginning of the Civil War, and had his Henry rifle, the first practical lever action repeater, available to the largely uninterested military during that conflict.

Today Winchester is known as the maker of the prototypical hunting rifle, the .30-30 used by countless deer hunters. The company has had a long and successful line of all kinds of sporting rifles and shotguns, in addition to producing many of the rifles and other shoulder arms which carried the U.S. Army through World Wars I and II.

The Winchester company has always been a pioneer in arms innovation. At the time it developed the first practical lever action repeating rifle, most shoulder arms were still primitive muzzleloaders. Later in the 1800s, the company formed an alliance with John Browning, who

invented the first high power repeating rifles used for big game hunting, notably by Theodore Roosevelt. The .22 caliber pump action rifle familiar from amusement park days and as a boy's first gun was also initiated by Winchester and Browning. In World War II, the famous M1 carbine was partly invented by a Winchester employee, ex-convict "Carbine Williams." All these arms share the quality of high esthetic appeal, which has also resulted in high prices for collectors of these arms.

Left: Portrait of company founder Oliver Fisher Winchester in his later years, by G. S. Hopkinson. Winchester's previous career was in shirtmaking, perhaps accounting for the handsome example here.

Right: When Horse Flesh Comes High, by Charles M. Russell, the author's favorite Western painter. Winchester Model 1873 rifle being fired by the cowboy in the foreground. (Courtesy of the Amon Carter Museum, Fort Worth, Texas.)

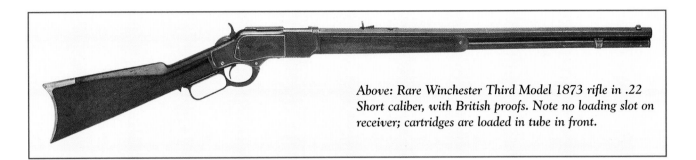

Above: Rare Winchester Third Model 1873 rifle in .22 Short caliber, with British proofs. Note no loading slot on receiver; cartridges are loaded in tube in front.

The company has had outstanding if sporadic commercial success. The invention of the Henry rifle and the later Browning patents gave the company a virtual monopoly on lever action arms as late as 1900, when at least 75 percent of the repeating sporting arms on the American market were made by Winchester. World War I, with major rifle contracts such as the British and the American Armies with the Enfield and the Russians with the 1895 Winchester, saw a huge expansion of the company's factory complex in New Haven, Connecticut. Subsequent hard times, with the company being bought by the Olin family's Western Cartridge Company in 1931, were succeeded by another period of expansion during World War II. A postwar slump was again followed by a change in ownership, to GIAT, owner of Browning Arms and Fabrique Nationale of Belgium (FN).

Today, as U.S. Repeating Arms Company, Inc., the company produces a full line of high quality sporting rifles and shotguns, with a modern factory on part of the original Winchester site in New Haven making the barrels, and other components being made on a multi-national basis. The Custom Shop also remains in New Haven. The Olin Corporation still retains trademark rights to the Winchester name, and also produces the Winchester ammunition. The proud tradition of Winchester and its arms continues.

The following chapters cover all the major varieties of arms produced under the Winchester (and before that Henry) name from 1860 to the present. The emphasis is less on technical details than on how and why the arms were developed, within their historical background, and the personalities of who made and used these arms. It is a

Above: Medicine Lodge, Kansas, citizens' posse (most with Winchesters) who captured Henry Newton Brown, marshal of Caldwell. He attempted to rob a bank, April 30, 1884, and was killed while trying to escape from the town jail.

Above right: The famous Winchester cowboy logo, still going strong, as shown in the company's Year 2000 catalog. The trademark is actually owned by the Olin Corporation, licensed to the U.S. Repeating Arms Company, the manufacturer today of Winchester firearms.

colorful story, reflecting the growth of the nation and of its industrial power. Winchester has become a part of American folklore.

The opening chapter tells the story of how Oliver Winchester, an industrialist with little previous knowledge of firearms, seized on a revolutionary firearms invention, the lever action repeating rifle, and made it a success, much as Samuel Colt did with the revolving pistol. This is intertwined with the story of arms development, or the lack of it, in the American Civil War. The second chapter describes the transition of the Civil War Henry rifle to the legendary Models 1866 and 1873, the fully evolved lever action rifles which became the predominant, or at least the most visible, of all the shoulder arms used in the Frontier West.

The third chapter explores Winchester's new development, with John Browning's help, of more

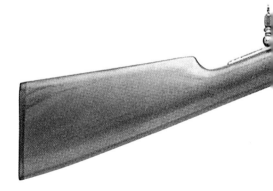

Above: Winchester Model 1890 slide action .22 caliber rifle, Third Model. A popular shooting gallery rifle, it was one of the best selling rimfire repeaters in Winchester history.

WINCHESTER
RIFLES AND SHOTGUNS
Licensee

powerful rifles for big game hunting, and also the company's entry into the field of shotguns for birds and smaller game. The fourth chapter has been provided by Philip Schreier, Manager of the National Rifle Association Gun Collector Programs, on Theodore Roosevelt and his Winchester hunting guns.

Chapter 5 relates the major role Winchester played in both World Wars I and II in developing and producing military rifles and shotguns. Together with other private manufacturers like Colt, Winchester formed an important part of the "Arsenal of Democracy." This is followed up by Chapter 6, Hunting and Sporting Arms Since the 1920s, describing Winchester's production of quality arms for

hunting and other shooting sports. It also considers the "gun control" issue as it may apply to the longarms made by Winchester. These are certainly not "assault weapons," but may potentially be affected by extension, in the debate over restrictions on handguns. The potential problem is also considered of lack of reserve facilities for the production of military smallarms.

Recognizing the great interest in Winchester among the large number of arms collectors, Chapter 7 includes a discussion of trends in prices (upward!) and means of starting or expanding a collection, such as through auctions, gun shows, and antique arms dealers. Also, opportunities to see examples of fine Winchesters are explored, in museums which often are not widely known.

Chapter 8 describes the power and accuracy characteristics of certain Winchester guns, partly based on firing a variety of early arms. Even antique Winchesters are seen to have to performed well for their intended use.

The basic sources of information about the history of Winchester arms, as listed in the Bibliography, are *The Winchester Book*, by George Madis; *Winchester, The Gun That Won the West*, by Harold F. Williamson; *Winchester Repeating Arms Company*, by Herbert G. Houze; *Evolution of the Winchester*, by R. Bruce McDowell, and *Winchester, An American Legend*, by R. L. Wilson. Beyond these, the author gratefully acknowledges the personal help of R. L. Wilson, who graciously received me in his Connecticut home and office; Philip Schreier of the National Rifle Association; and Angus Laidlaw, a contributing editor of *American Rifleman* magazine. The Winchester staff at the "Shot Show" in Las Vegas, Nevada, in January, 2000, were also particularly helpful, as has been, in the collecting field, Greg Martin, Director of Arms and Armor at Butterfield and Butterfield, auctioneers and appraisers in San Francisco, who permitted the use of some photographs of firearms which appeared in their catalogs, and Martin Lane of the Martin Lane Historical Americana Gallery in New York. The work done by Anne Lang of Picture Research and Archives of Arlington, Virginia, in collecting the book's illustrations, is also appreciated. R. L. Wilson and his outstanding photographer, G. Allan Brown, kindly gave permission for the reproduction of some photographs from *Winchester, An American Legend*.

THE BEGINNINGS:
THE HENRY RIFLE

The first real Winchester rifle, produced by Oliver Fisher Winchester's New Haven Arms Company, was the Henry. Patented in 1860 and produced in 1862, in time for use during the Civil War of 1861 to 1865, this rifle was amazingly modern in all of its details except for its front loading magazine. Its key feature was the two-piece "toggle link" connecting the lever, the hammer, the bolt containing the firing pins, and the movable carrier which brought the cartridges from the magazine under the barrel to a position at the mouth of the chamber in the barrel. This allowed rapid fire, with a full 15-shot magazine emptied in only 10.8 seconds in a Civil War trial, and this magazine capacity was such that it was referred to in Civil War correspondence as "the gun that was loaded on Sunday and fired all week."

This revolutionary new development can be better appreciated in comparison with other arms of the time. The U.S. Army in 1860 was in the process of adopting Samuel Colt's six-shot revolver in .44 caliber as the standard sidearm, representing a comparable advance in handgun technology. However, in regard to the mainstay of the infantry, the rifle musket, the Ordnance Department was firmly wedded to the single-shot muzzleloading Springfield type, in which for each shot, the soldier had to bite off the end of a paper cartridge, pour the powder in the muzzle, insert the bullet with a ramrod, cock the hammer, and place a percussion cap on the nipple under the hammer, before he could aim and fire.

More advanced rifles had been developed, but each had disadvantages. Colt's revolving military rifle was a five-shot repeater, but each chamber had to be loaded individually with loose powder and ball and individual percussion caps affixed, in addition to which power was reduced by gas escaping between the cylinder and the barrel. Also, the possibility of multiple firing between cylinders put the user's hand at risk in holding the barrel in front of the cylinder.

The Sharps rifle was an excellent breechloader, but only single-shot, and again without a self-contained cartridge. The Spencer, with a seven-shot magazine loading through the butt and with a .52 caliber rimfire cartridge, was the nearest approach to the Winchester, but required cocking the hammer by hand for each shot, in addition to working the lever to advance the cartridge.

Europe, perhaps due to a series of wars in the first half of the 1800s, was temporarily ahead of the United States in developing breechloading rifles and the self-contained cartridge. The Dreyse Needle Gun was adopted by the Prussian Army in 1840. Under this system, the firing pin was driven through the cartridge into a primer located at the base of the bullet. Lefaucheux in France developed the successful pinfire cartridge for shotguns and pistols, completely self-contained and fired by means of a pin forming a part of the cartridge, extending at right angles to the base of the cartridge. Again in France, Flobert developed a small rimfire cartridge in which the primer also served as the propellant. However, these were still primitive, compared to the Henry rifle and its .44 caliber rimfire cartridge.

The period before 1860, when the Henry was patented, was propitious in the United States for the development of new firearms. As a largely pioneer and agrarian society before that time, Americans had always been familiar with firearms (although there is some present dispute on this, by "gun control" advocates). Professor Harold Williamson, in *Winchester, The Gun That Won The West*, illustrates this background as follows:

"Firearms, the axe and the plow were the three cornerstones upon which the pioneer Americans built this nation. Of the three, firearms were the most dramatic and appealed most to popular imagination. The musket or rifle was a necessity for the pioneer who depended upon his ability as a marksman to provide food and clothing and to protect himself against attack. By 1774 a visiting Englishman could write, 'There is not a Man born in America that does not Understand the Use of Firearms and that well . . . it is Almost the First thing they Purchase and take to all the New Settlements and in the Cities you can scarcely find a Lad of 12 years that does not go a Gunning.'"

After the War of 1812 there was little call for the American armed forces outside of sporadic engagements with the Native Americans, notably the Seminole War of 1838, until the Mexican War of 1846 to 1848. That followed the formation of the State of Texas and its repulse of the Mexican dictator Santa Anna after the fall of the Alamo. In these engagements with Mexico, where the Mexican Army began with about 30,000 men as against the American military establishment of 5,000, the value of repeating arms became evident, at least to the Texans, who made good use of Colt's repeating rifles and pistols.

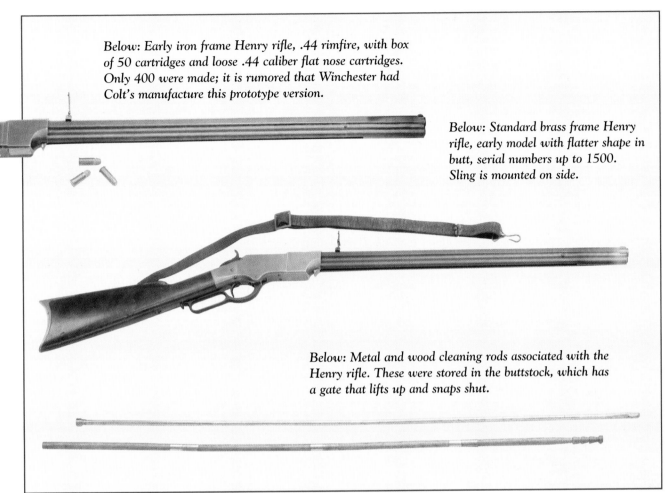

Below: Early iron frame Henry rifle, .44 rimfire, with box of 50 cartridges and loose .44 caliber flat nose cartridges. Only 400 were made; it is rumored that Winchester had Colt's manufacture this prototype version.

Below: Standard brass frame Henry rifle, early model with flatter shape in butt, serial numbers up to 1500. Sling is mounted on side.

Below: Metal and wood cleaning rods associated with the Henry rifle. These were stored in the buttstock, which has a gate that lifts up and snaps shut.

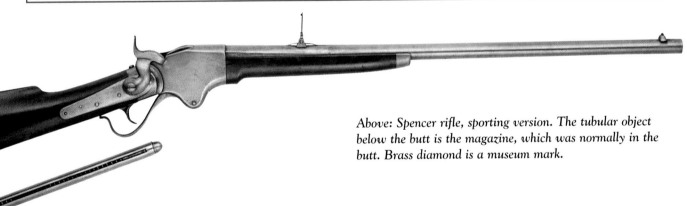

Above: Spencer rifle, sporting version. The tubular object below the butt is the magazine, which was normally in the butt. Brass diamond is a museum mark.

Below: Breech mechanism of the Spencer in the loading position. The return of the lever will force the next round into the chamber

Below: Spencer breech closed and hammer cocked ready for firing. Sporting versions using more powerful cartridges were also made but were not popular.

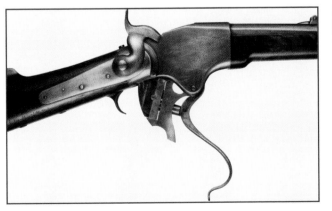

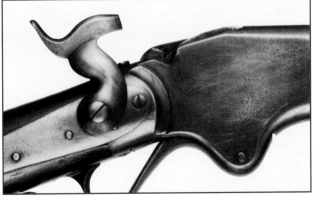

At the same time, the American expansion westward had become a stampede, especially after the discovery of gold in California in 1849. There was an insatiable demand for firearms by the pioneers and miners for hunting, defense against Native Americans, and for self protection against lawless elements. Worldwide, expansion of frontiers was also proceeding, such as in South America and Australia.

Part of the background of the Henry rifle is the new technology which made its production possible, and which attracted Oliver Winchester and later the famous Horace Smith and Daniel Wesson to the companies which made the predecessors to the Henry. This was the "American System" of mass production by machine, allowing interchangeable parts for products including firearms. This engendered specialization of labor, in which, instead of a skilled gunsmith making an entire gun, less skilled workmen could use machines to work just on separate parts. A comparable advance in its time to present-day computerized technology, this opened new opportunities for venture capitalists, including Oliver Winchester.

The impetus for precision machine manufacturing in the United States was related in large part to the need for firearms. As early as 1798 the Federal Government established two National Armories, in Springfield, Massachusetts, and Harper's Ferry, Virginia. As well as developing and producing smallarms for the military, the Springfield Armory in particular developed a system of new machine tools and inspection for private contractors producing military arms, who themselves were encouraged to innovate. Eli Whitney in New Haven and Simeon North in Berlin and then Middletown, Connecticut, experimented with but did not quite achieve interchangeability of parts. Additional efforts were made by John Hall of Maine, who was called to Harper's Ferry to supervise the manufacture of the breechloading flintlock rifle he had invented, somewhat ahead of its time. A major breakthrough was made in 1844 at the Robbins, Kendall and Lawrence factory in Windsor, Vermont, where new machinery was designed and made so effectively that a contract for 10,000 Harper's Ferry type U.S. Army rifles was completed

Above: Jennings pill primer repeating rifle. With its predecessor the Hunt, this was the first lever action repeater. It is so scarce that Flayderman's Guide To Antique American Firearms says, "no known sales in recent times."

Above: Pair of Hunt's patented .54 caliber "rocket balls."

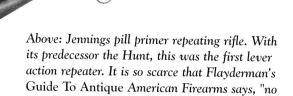

Left: Typical scene after the discovery of gold in California in 1849, which produced a rush of new population in the State and an accompanying market for firearms.

18 months ahead of schedule, with further orders following. This pioneering factory, which is still preserved as the American Precision Museum, produced the second of the three longarms which led to the Henry rifle: the Hunt, the Jennings, and the Volcanic.

The Hunt, of which only one example survives, was invented and patented by Walter Hunt in New York in 1849. It used a hollow-based conical bullet which he called the "Rocket Ball," filled with powder and with the base closed by a cork wad having a hole in its center to admit the flame from an independent priming unit he had patented in 1848. It was called the "Volitional Repeater," and incorporated the combination of a straight spring-driven firing pin and a tubular magazine under the barrel, which became features of the Henry and Winchester rifles. Hunt was a brilliant inventor who was never able to capitalize on his diverse inventions such as the safety pin and the lock-stitch needle which became the basis for the sewing machine. He was not able to finance the development of the "Volitional Repeater" either, and sold his rights to a fellow New Yorker, George A. Arrowsmith, a modelmaker and machinist. He in turn had his employee Lewis Jennings simplify the repeating mechanism, the result of which was patented at the end of 1849. At this point, with the help of Courtland Palmer, a leading hardware merchant in New York, an order was placed with the Robbins and Lawrence factory to have 5,000 Jennings patent rifles produced.

Here two names which were to become famous entered the picture. Daniel Wesson, an experienced gunsmith, was working at Robbins and Lawrence, and proceeded with experimental work on the Jennings mechanism, at Palmer's request. Horace Smith, another experienced gunsmith, was also engaged to help develop the new repeating rifle. Working out of Norwich, Connecticut, he had already begun making the .22 caliber Flobert pistol developed in France, using its primitive form of rimfire cartridge. While the Jennings rifle was still too complicated and underpowered for commercial success, Smith and Wesson with Palmer's support continued experimentation, and in 1854 patented an effective mechanism for moving the carrier and locking it in its forward position, which completed the essential mechanical features of the Henry and Winchester rifles.

The rifle did not sell well and production was curtailed. Only a few Jennings rifles were produced as repeaters, with an automatic pill primer mechanism. The rest of the production of less than 1,000 was in the configuration of a breechloading single-shot rifle in .54 caliber, but still using the "Rocket Ball" cartridge and the automatic pill primer (a wafer with primer inserted onto a percussion nipple by the action of the hammer). After the improvements by Horace Smith at the Robbins and Lawrence factory, three more models were produced, this time all as repeaters, referred to as the Smith-Jennings rifle.

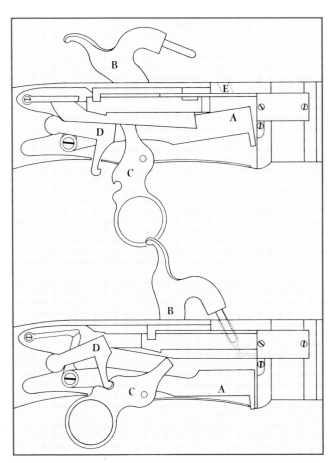

Above: Jennings breech mechanisms: upper one ready to fire. A round has been lifted on the scoop-shaped carrier (A) and chambered; the hammer (B) is cocked and ready to strike a percussion pill in the aperture (E). After firing, the trigger (C) is drawn back to engage the lock (D) and drop the carrier for a new round

Below: Jennings rifle cocked and ready to fire. The long striker nose, the pill container, and the pill aperture are all clearly shown.

Bottom: Jennings with hammer down.

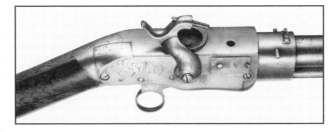

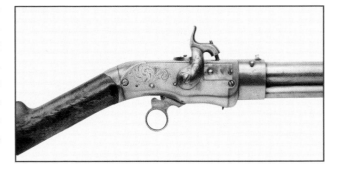

Smith and Wesson then formed a partnership, together with Courtland Palmer, under the name of Smith & Wesson Manufacturing in Norwich, Connecticut. But, presaging the future, the company concentrated on producing pistols with the new repeating mechanism. Recognizing that the ammunition with the powder inside the bullet was not very effective, Smith patented an inside-primed, centerfire, metal cartridge, but it is a mystery why this promising approach was not pursued. In the meantime, in 1855, a year after the partnership was formed, a buyout offer was made by a group of New Haven and New York investors including Oliver Winchester, which was accepted. Smith and Wesson then moved to Springfield, Massachusetts, where they pursued the development of revolving pistols, with the successful results still apparent today in the Smith & Wesson Company.

The total production by Smith & Wesson Manufacturing in Norwich was about 1,700, all of repeating pistols. Approximately 1,200 were in .31 caliber with bag shaped grips, and under 500 were in .41 caliber. All had steel frames,

with the barrel marking "SMITH & WESSON, NORWICH, CT., PATENTED FEB. 14, 1854, CAST STEEL."

When the new company was formed as the Volcanic Repeating Arms Company, Oliver Winchester had 80 of the 6,000 shares. Evidently Winchester was attracted by the glamor and potential of the new invention, much as venture capitalists today invest in Internet companies, not necessarily knowing much about the company's products.

Winchester, forty-six years old at the time he made his investment in the Volcanic Repeating Arms Company, was already a successful industrialist. Like Samuel Colt, he had a difficult childhood. His father, a Massachusetts farmer, died a year after Oliver and twin brother Samuel were born, and his mother was left with very little with which to raise and educate her children. Young Oliver had to go to work on a farm at the age of seven. He was apprenticed to a carpenter at the age of 14 and became a master builder at the age of 20, when he moved to Baltimore and became a building contractor. In 1833, with a wife followed by three children,

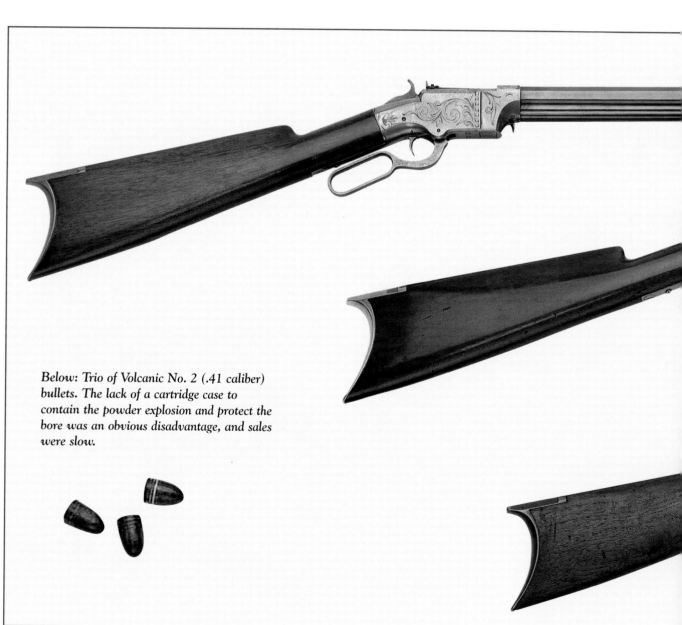

Below: Trio of Volcanic No. 2 (.41 caliber) bullets. The lack of a cartridge case to contain the powder explosion and protect the bore was an obvious disadvantage, and sales were slow.

he went into the men's clothing business, opening a small retail store and then a larger downtown store. In 1847, he patented an improvement in the manufacture of men's dress shirts. During the subsequent three years he moved to New Haven, took on a partner, John Davies, a leading importer and jobber of men's clothing in New York, and developed a flourishing factory in New Haven which by 1860 employed 40 male and 1,500 female workers, most working at home under contract. His management of the shirt factory continued until 1866, when he went full time into the firearms manufacturing business.

The Volcanic Repeating Arms Company lasted only from June 1855 to February 1857. Its production consisted only of some 3,000 lever action pistols in .41 caliber, mainly with 6 inch and 8 inch barrels. There were some 300 made into carbines with 16 inch barrels and attached shoulder stocks. The standard barrel marking was "THE VOLCANIC REPEATING ARMS CO. NEW HAVEN CONN. PAT FEB. 14, 1854."

The name "Volcanic" originated as a nickname for the previous Smith & Wesson pistol type arms. According to Roy Jinks, the Smith & Wesson historian, it came from an article in *Scientific American* magazine in 1854, comparing the rapid fire capability of the gun with the fiery eruption of a volcano.

Although Smith, Wesson, and Palmer received 2,800 shares of a total of 65,000 shares of stock in the Volcanic Company, and Smith remained as general manager during the latter part of 1855 before the company moved to New Haven in early 1856, none of the three appears to have taken an active part in the company. A new manager was hired, William C. Hicks, an experienced mechanic but with no experience in guns. The president of the company, Nelson B. Gaston, had made his fortune in minerals and shipping. Oliver Winchester was vice president, and then, when Gaston suddenly died in December 1856, unexpectedly became president.

A very substantial arms factory, for its time, was

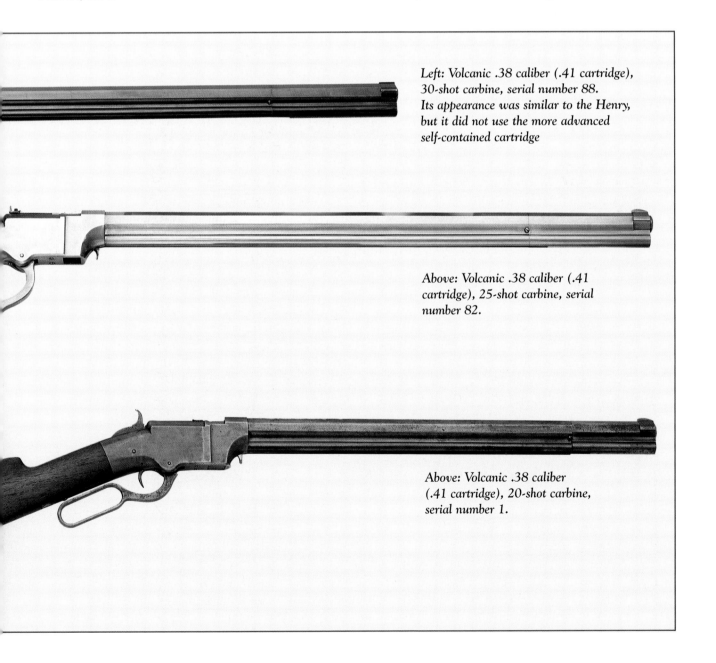

Left: Volcanic .38 caliber (.41 cartridge), 30-shot carbine, serial number 88. Its appearance was similar to the Henry, but it did not use the more advanced self-contained cartridge

Above: Volcanic .38 caliber (.41 cartridge), 25-shot carbine, serial number 82.

Above: Volcanic .38 caliber (.41 cartridge), 20-shot carbine, serial number 1.

established, with a labor force of some 50 employees, including four girls making ammunition. There was a heavy investment in machinery and equipment, in the new tradition of the "American System" of production. Professor Harold Williamson comments that while outside suppliers provided frames and receivers made of brass castings, drilled gun barrels of mild steel, and rough gun stocks, "otherwise the quantity and variety of machinery on hand was extensive enough to have produced practically all of the parts that went into the finished products, plus the making of gauges, jigs, and fixtures."

Williamson also comments that the company's attention seems to have been focused on financing and manufacturing problems, and because of inexperience ignored the futility of staying with the faulty "Rocket Ball" ammunition. The company also had a lack of sufficient working capital and a

Above: New Haven Arms Co. plant, as seen in 1859. The figure in the window is supposedly Oliver Winchester.

Top: Photograph of Oliver Fisher Winchester, without beard (as shown in his portrait on page 8). He clearly had a commanding presence

problem of quality control in manufacturing (a lawsuit was brought by a major distributor because of defective arms received). However, from a present-day perspective, it is understandable that the participants would have been dazzled by the potential of the new mechanical system for a repeating firearm.

Starting in the spring of 1856, Winchester and Gaston began making substantial loans to the Volcanic Company for working capital. However, this was not enough, and in February, 1857, the company was unable to pay notes which fell due from the Tradesman's Bank of New Haven, and was declared bankrupt. It is interesting that Eli Whitney, Jr., who had continued his father's substantial Whitney Armory, a major New Haven gun manufacturer (Eli Whitney, Sr., was best known as the inventor of the cotton gin as a young man), was one of the appraisers appointed by the Court.

Above: Benjamin Tyler Henry, who developed and gave his name to the Henry rifle, but who later tried to take the company away from Winchester.

Winchester arranged with the heirs of Gaston, who had died in December, to take over their claims, and the entire assets of the company were turned over to Winchester. He received all of the company's property, including the machinery, patents, and guns in process, for the amount of about $40,000. While this was a substantial amount of money for the time, it was only the amount that Winchester had loaned the company, meaning that he had eliminated the other stockholders' interest at no real further cost to himself.

The New Haven Arms Company

The successor to the Volcanic Repeating Arms Company was formed as The New Haven Arms Company in late 1857. Oliver Winchester further demonstrated his business acumen and salesmanship by assembling 11 investors for the company's 2,000 shares of stock, of which he held a controlling interest of 800 shares. Seven of the investors had owned stock in the failed Volcanic Company. Winchester received his stock in exchange for his interest in the previous company, plus $20,000 in cash which further reduced his original Volcanic investment. He still retained ownership of

the patents on the repeating gun mechanism.

The company continued the production of the Volcanic line of pistols and revolvers, only changing the barrel marking to drop the name Volcanic, and to refer to the patent as follows: "PATENT FEB. 14, 1854 – NEW HAVEN, CONN." The types and quantities were as follows:

Lever Action No. 1 Pocket Pistol, .31 caliber, 3½ inch and 6 inch barrels; quantity approximately 1,000.

Lever Action No. 2 Navy Pistol, .41 caliber, 8 inch and 6 inch barrels; quantity approximately 1,300. Also a few with a 16 inch barrel and attachable shoulder stock.

Lever Action Carbine, .41 caliber, 16½ inch, 21 inch, and 25 inch barrels; quantity approximately 1,000.

Sales were slow up until 1861, with solvency maintained through the personal credit of Winchester and his partner in the New Haven Shirt Manufacturing Company, John M. Davies. However, in a stroke of genius, Winchester brought in a new plant superintendent the year after the new company was formed, Benjamin Tyler Henry. Then 37 years old, 11 years younger than Winchester, Henry had worked in various gun workshops from age 16, including the Springfield Armory, and at Robbins and Lawrence starting in 1842. He was that pioneering company's resident gun expert at the time that Smith, Wesson, and Palmer ordered the Jennings rifle and supervised its development into the Volcanic.

Finally recognizing that the key to turning the Volcanic into a practical repeating rifle was its cartridge, Winchester had Henry start work on developing what became the .44 caliber cartridge and the Henry rifle. Also recognizing that the future of the lever action arms lay in rifles rather than pistols, Winchester had the company concentrate exclusively on rifles except for a short term contract to produce 3,000 .31 caliber Walch pocket model revolvers for Cyrus Manville of New York City. This was an open top 10-shot revolver with a superposed load. Walch was one of a series of inventors who tried unsuccessfully to compete with Colt upon the expiration of the Colt revolver patent in 1857.

By 1859 Henry had developed a .38 caliber cartridge, but Winchester saw this would be too light, and by 1860 Henry perfected the .44 caliber cartridge. At the same time, Henry redesigned the Volcanic rifle to use this cartridge, and the patent for the new rifle, which Winchester was glad to call the Henry, was issued on October 16, 1860. It is interesting to note that the successors to Winchester's company have all honored the name of Henry by inscribing the letter H on the base of all rimfire cartridges, now only in.22 caliber, up to the present time.

However, the terms of Henry's pay appear to have led to dissension between Henry and Oliver Winchester. Henry was hired in 1858 at a salary of $1,500 per year, but in 1859 this was changed to a contract under which he was to employ the workers and provide the supplies to manufacture 5,000 arms, at a fixed price to be paid by the company. This is an example of the inside contract system which was widely used by manufacturers at the time, under which factory foremen

would contract for the production, leaving the management to provide materials and handle financing and sales. (An advantage of this system, which lasted until the late 1800s, was that apprentices could work their way up under the direct tutelage of skilled mechanics, and innovation was encouraged.) It is interesting that some modern industries are returning to the idea of decentralizing authority, although in a generally different form.) The result for Henry was that during the five year contract period he made about twice the amount he would have made with his previous salary, but this was not a generous payment for the inventions which led to the company's and Oliver Winchester's great fortunes.

Henry's retaliation was, according to Professor Williamson, that "he never substantially increased the work force under his control even when the company had purchased additional machinery when orders warranted increased production." Winchester was understandably

Above: Iron frame Model 1860 Henry rifle, with serial number 2 on barrel and 41 on frame, stock and buttplate. When offered for auction, the estimated price was $35,000 to $40,000.

THE HENRY RIFLE

Type: 15-shot lever action rifle.
Made: 1860–1866.

Variations: Iron Frame Model, separate serial numbers 1 to 400, may have been made at Colt's in Hartford; Early Brass Frame Model, serial numbers 1 to 1,500; Late Brass Frame Model, heel of the buttplate has a pointed profile.

Quantity: Total approximately 14,000, including Civil War government purchases of 1,731.

Caliber: .44 rimfire.

Barrel length: 24 1/4 inches. A few experimental models made with shortened barrels, and some shortened by users to reduce weight of 9 1/4 pounds.

Markings: On the top of the barrel, plus serial number; HENRY'S PATENT OCT. 16, 1860, MANUFACT'D BY THE NEWHAVEN ARMS CO., NEWHAVEN CT. Some with inspector's marks on lower tang and elsewhere, H for B. Tyler Henry and W for Oliver Winchester. Barrel and lever finished bright blue; frame, sideplates, and buttplate polished brass; hammer and

trigger casehardened. A few decorated by engraving at factory; some others engraved by dealers or users (some engraving reportedly modern). Henry, and late Model 1866, frames were actually made of a bronze alloy, primarily copper and tin, for greater strength. However, "brass" is the usual term used in the literature and by collectors, so is used also in this book, although brass is made primarily of copper and zinc.

Mechanical function: Lever action, in which moving the lever forward to a position perpendicular to the rifle cocks the hammer, ejects the empty cartridge if present, and raises the carrier inside the frame so that it brings a fresh cartridge from the magazine under the barrel into alignment with the chamber. Bringing the lever back again pushes and locks the fresh cartridge into the chamber. There are two firing pins which engage opposite sides of the rimfire cartridge. The magazine under the barrel is loaded from the front, after turning a revolving block attached to the front of the barrel; the cartridges are held by a follower and spring inside the magazine tube. The principle is the same for all subsequent lever action rifles, except that, after the Henry, loading the cartridges took place from a gate on the side of the frame, at the rear of the magazine.

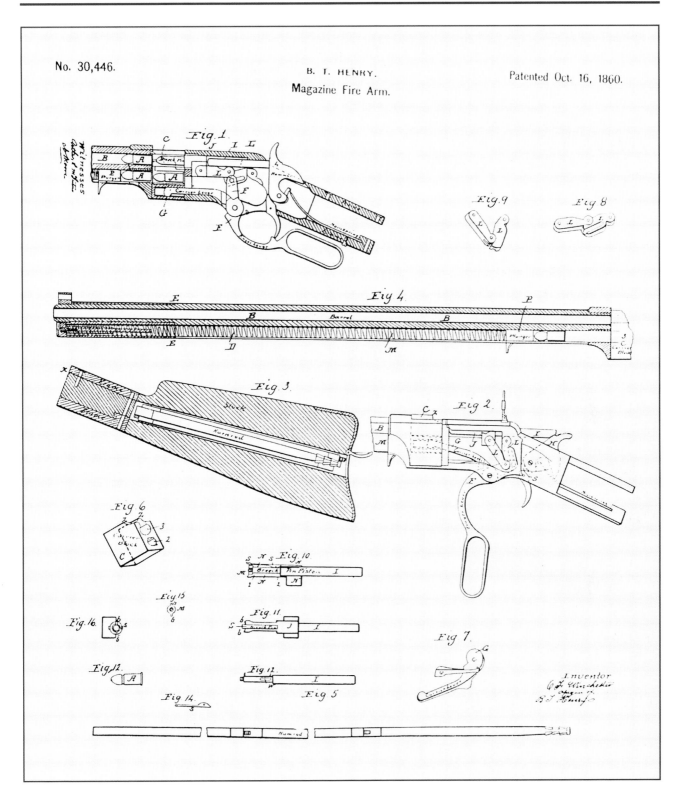

No. 30,446.

B. T. HENRY.
Magazine Fire Arm.

Patented Oct. 16, 1860.

frustrated by delays in delivery of the rifles, and in December 1863 he personally leased a building in Bridgeport, Connecticut, and purchased machinery for it so that Henry rifle production could be increased as soon as the contract with Henry expired in 1864. At that point Henry left the company, and new superintendents were engaged for both the New Haven and Bridgeport factories. The total work force was increased from 37 to 100, of which 37 were women engaged in making cartridges.

Henry again tried to retaliate at the end of the Civil War in 1865, when Winchester decided to retire from the shirt

Above: Patent and drawing for the Henry rifle, 1860. This shows the toggle link mechanism which was carried forward with Winchester rifles until the Model 1886 design by John Browning.

making business and take an extended trip to Europe. While Winchester was on this trip, Henry, who was still a stockholder in the company, petitioned the Connecticut State Legislature to change the name of the company to the Henry Repeating Rifle Company, and to have the stockholders turn its control over to him. Enraged,

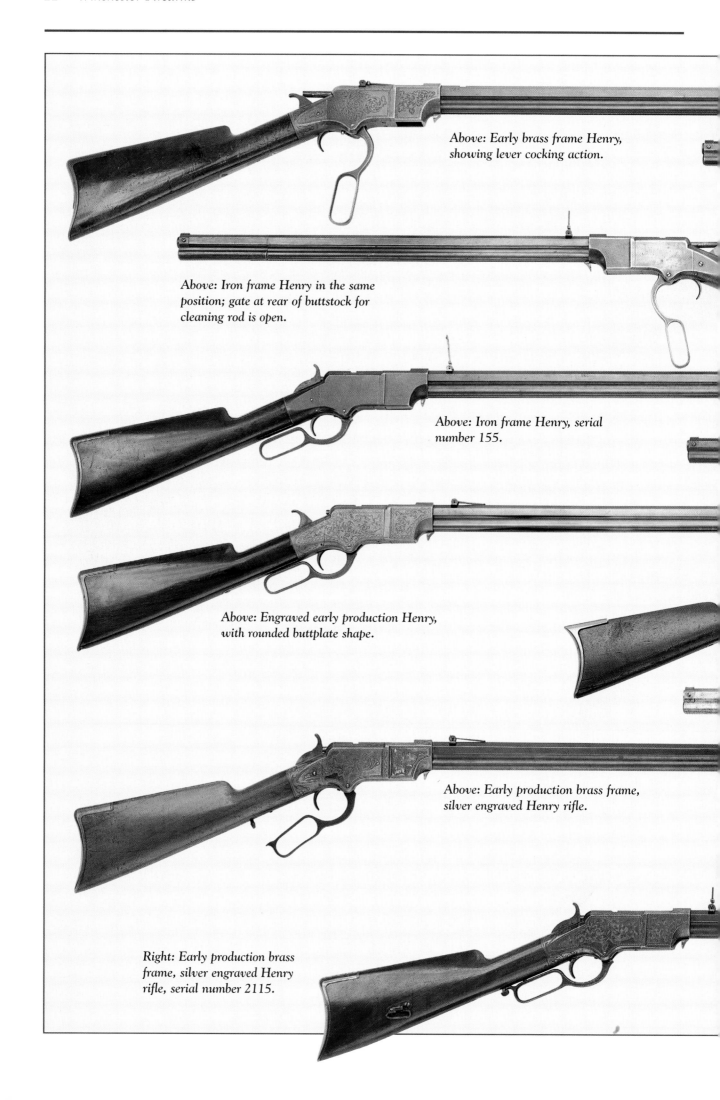

Above: Early brass frame Henry, showing lever cocking action.

Above: Iron frame Henry in the same position; gate at rear of buttstock for cleaning rod is open.

Above: Iron frame Henry, serial number 155.

Above: Engraved early production Henry, with rounded buttplate shape.

Above: Early production brass frame, silver engraved Henry rifle.

Right: Early production brass frame, silver engraved Henry rifle, serial number 2115.

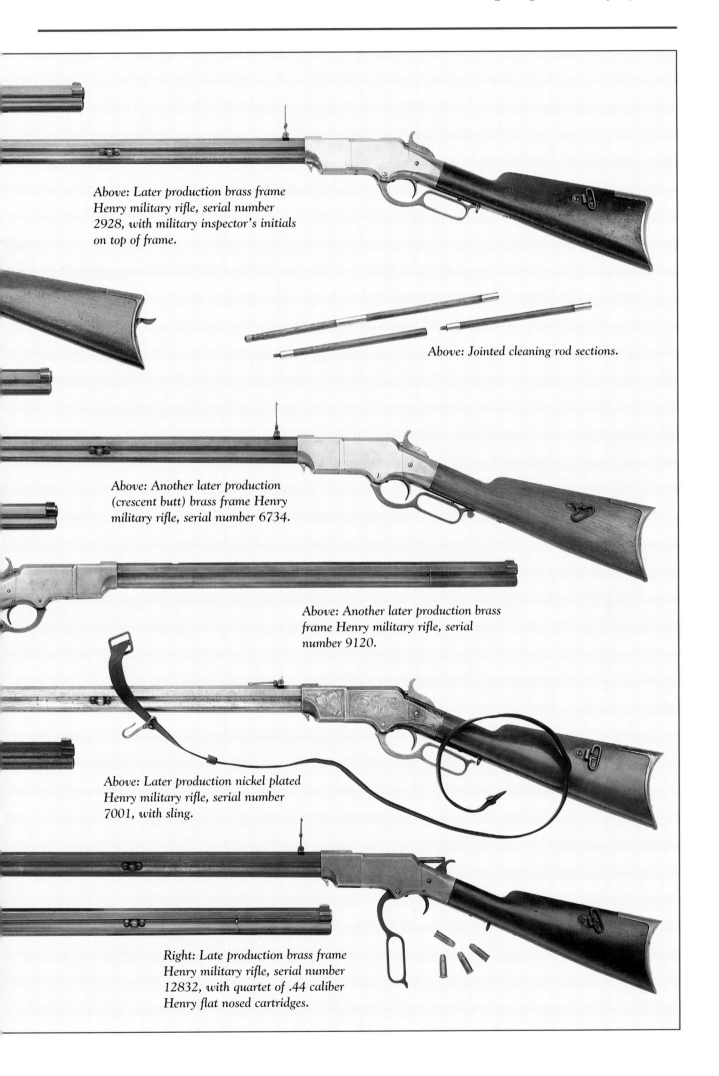

Above: Later production brass frame Henry military rifle, serial number 2928, with military inspector's initials on top of frame.

Above: Jointed cleaning rod sections.

Above: Another later production (crescent butt) brass frame Henry military rifle, serial number 6734.

Above: Another later production brass frame Henry military rifle, serial number 9120.

Above: Later production nickel plated Henry military rifle, serial number 7001, with sling.

Right: Late production brass frame Henry military rifle, serial number 12832, with quartet of .44 caliber Henry flat nosed cartridges.

Winchester returned to New Haven and effectively thwarted this attempted takeover. He formed a new company with added investors and, with the original investors participating, called it the Winchester Repeating Arms Company. His partner Davies remained loyal and later became a multimillionaire along with Winchester, from his holdings in the company's stock.

Henry rifle in the Civil War

Upon the firing on Fort Sumter opening the Civil War in the spring of 1861, Oliver Winchester was not yet prepared for mass production of the Henry rifle, but there is indirect evidence, based on invoices from the Colt Armory, that he immediately had Colt's factory in Hartford produce his first 400 rifles, which had an iron frame rather than brass. These are now the rarest of the
Henrys, valued at over $70,000 on the collectors' market.

By the spring of 1862, the standard brass frame Henrys were being offered on the commercial market, and Oliver Winchester was making strenuous efforts to sell the new arm to the U.S. Ordnance Department. A Navy trial in May 1862 produced the enthusiastic finding that firing could be done with one shot every 2.9 seconds, as compared with the best performance of a muzzleloader at one shot each 20 seconds. For accuracy and range, a shooter of average ability
placed 14 out of 15 shots in a target 18 inch square at distance of 348 feet.

Eventually, starting in 1863, the Ordnance Department

Below: Late production .44 caliber Henry rifle.
The cartridges are now collectors' items; Winchester's cartridge business expanded as production increased with later models.

bought 1,731 Henry rifles, and there were State and private purchases of another 8,372 for military use, but this is a very small number compared with the 1.5 million muzzleloading rifle muskets bought by the Ordnance Department during the war. Other repeating and breechloading rifles were bought in somewhat greater quantity, especially in the form of cavalry carbines, since it was difficult to argue that muzzleloaders could be used on horseback. Some 130,000 Spencer repeating rifles and carbines, 115,000 Sharps rifles and carbines, and 8,500 Colt revolving rifles were used by the Union forces, but this was still a small number compared with the standard muzzleloaders.

It is tempting to speculate by how much the Civil War would have been shortened if the Union had seized the opportunity which might have been provided by the Henry rifle. The weapon did have shortcomings: its light .38 caliber cartridge had only about half the muzzle energy of the .58 caliber infantry musket (see the chapter on firing). Its mechanism was delicate and subject to malfunction through dirt entering the open action and the open slot under the tubular magazine; by the magazine being dented; and by the revolving block in front of the magazine being jammed. It was not adaptable to the bayonet, (although its weight would have made it useful as a club).

On the other hand, its advantages were potentially overwhelming. Most soldiers, in the Civil War (and since), shot effectively only at ranges not much over 100 yards, and the Henry's short range firepower would have been devastating to the massed armies of the Civil War, as well as providing "assault rifle" capabilities for storming defensive positions. Also, and very importantly, the Confederates did not have the technology to manufacture the cartridges, so could not have matched the Henry's firepower even if they had been able to capture large numbers of arms, as they did with the North's rifle muskets.

THE HENRY CARTRIDGE

Caliber: .44, drawn copper with a swaged rim on the base containing fulminate as the primer. Letter H on bottom for B. Tyler Henry.

Bullet: 200 to 216 grains lead, originally round nosed and then with flattened head; grooves around the base of the bullet for adding tallow to prevent fouling of the gun bore. Black powder charge 26 to 28 grains.

Muzzle velocity: 1,200 feet per second. This compares with the Volcanic "Rocket Ball" of less than 500 feet per second; that

cartridge had the powder in the hollow base of the bullet. It did not seal off the gas from the explosion, as the copper cartridge did by expansion or obturation.

Daniel Wesson developed a smaller cartridge on this principle in 1858 which was used in the Smith & Wesson .22 and .32 caliber pistols, and patented this in 1860, but that did not prevent Winchester from using the Henry cartridge. He claimed it was covered under his Volcanic patents, and Wesson did not contest this claim.

The lack of interest shown by the Ordnance Department in Oliver Winchester's attempts to sell the Henry – he wrote offering to provide an initial amount of 40,000 rifles – was only part of a larger failure to appreciate what even a modest change in the infantry rifle could have done, from a muzzleloader to a breechloader. Professor Robert V. Bruce of Boston University published a book in 1956, *Lincoln And The Tools Of War*, in which he developed this theme, ending with a definite and startling conclusion. His two protagonists are President Abraham Lincoln, who understood the technology of his time and after a famous personal trial of the Spencer repeating rifle succeeded in having it adopted on a limited

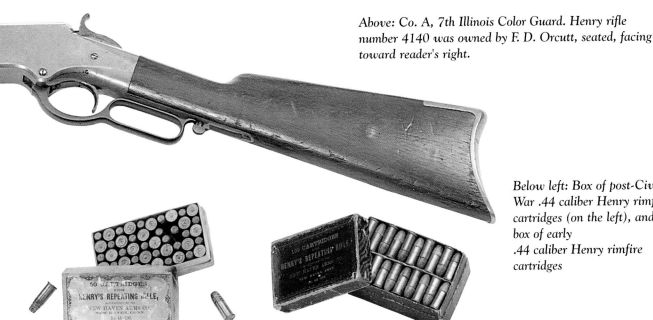

Above: Co. A, 7th Illinois Color Guard. Henry rifle number 4140 was owned by F. D. Orcutt, seated, facing toward reader's right.

Below left: Box of post-Civil War .44 caliber Henry rimfire cartridges (on the left), and a box of early .44 caliber Henry rimfire cartridges

basis, and Brigadier General James W. Ripley, the elderly Chief of Ordnance, who stoutly resisted all attempts at innovation. Ripley expressed his credo as follows:

"A great evil now especially prevalent in regard to arms for the military service is the vast variety of the new inventions, each having, of course, its advocates, insisting on the superiority of his favorite arm over all others and urging its adoption by the Government. The influence thus exercised has already introduced into the service many kinds and calibers of arms, some, in my opinion, unfit for use as military weapons, and none as good as the U.S. musket, producing confusion in the manufacture, the issue, and the use of ammunition, and very injurious to the efficiency of troops. This evil can only be stopped by positively refusing to answer any requisitions for or propositions to sell new and untried arms, and steadily adhering to the rule of uniformity of arms for all troops of the same kind, such as cavalry, artillery, infantry."

Lincoln, on the other hand, test fired both single-shot breechloaders and repeating rifles in person, and was a frequent visitor to the Washington Navy Yard, where Admiral Dahlgren shared his views and promoted innovations in naval gunnery. It is notable that it was the Navy that conducted the first test of the Henry rifle for military use.

The case for the breechloading rifle was so obvious that even the Confederate President Jefferson Davis and Secretary of War John B. Floyd had recommended its adoption, when they each served as Secretaries of War for the United States government before the Civil War. Professor Bruce, referring to the field at Gettysburg at which 18,000 of the 24,000 loaded rifles and muskets found after the battle had two or more loads put into them by excited soldiers, making them inoperative, puts the case for breechloaders as follows:

"The obvious solution was a gun which could be loaded at the breech. At a stroke, almost all the pitfalls and complexities of loading would be eliminated. The soldier with a breechloader could not, even if he tried, put in more than one load at a time. He would not have to worry about a ramrod in loading. He could lie prone and load just as rapidly and easily as when he was standing. Not only would loading be gloriously simple, but breech-loading rifles would be better than muzzle-loaders in range and accuracy also, since tighter-fitting bullets could be used. And with such advantages would come the priceless asset of confidence, especially in the face of an enemy armed with only muzzle-loaders."

Finally, Professor Bruce expresses a definite opinion on how the Civil War might have ended:

"If by 1860 Davis and Floyd had carried their point, if they had adopted a regulation breechloader and had begun converting the Springfield Armory to its production, how different the course of history would have been! An able and intelligent Confederate general who encountered Yankee breechloaders during the war later maintained that the Confederacy would have gone down within a year had Federal infantry been thus armed at the start. Conversion begun as late as 1860 may not, probably would not, have been complete when war came. But if a large part of the Union Army had been given breechloaders by late 1862, Gettysburg would certainly have ended the war. More likely, Chancellorsville or even Fredericksburg would have done it, and history would record no Gettysburg Address, no President Grant, perhaps no carpetbag reconstruction or Solid South. Instead, it might have had the memoirs of ex-President Lincoln, perhaps written in retirement during the administration of President Burnside or Hooker."

If all this might have been accomplished by a single-shot breechloader, it is still more interesting to contemplate what the adoption of Henry's 16-shot repeater might have done (15 rounds in the magazine plus one in the chamber). A comparison suggests itself with the long delayed and acrimonious adoption in 1965 by the U.S. Army of Colt's AR-15 as the M16 automatic rifle, finally recognizing that it is firepower applied in the right place and at the right time which wins battles. The rifle it replaced, the .30 caliber Garand, had only an eight-shot magazine and was only semiautomatic, requiring the trigger to be pulled for each shot,while the M16, has a 30-round capacity with full automatic capability, at .228 caliber.

Effectiveness of the Henry

Despite its limited use in the Civil War, there were impressive reports of the effectiveness of the Henry rifle. Some of these reports were generated by Winchester himself, such as in his 1863 catalog, in which such stories are told as that of Captain James M. Wilson of the 12th Kentucky Cavalry, early in the war. Wilson was described as "an unconditional Union man, living in a strongly disloyal section of Kentucky." While he was at home dining with his family, seven Southern guerrillas rode up, dismounted, and burst into his dining room, firing revolvers. Captain Wilson sprang to his feet, exclaiming "for God's sake, gentlemen, if you wish to murder me, do not do

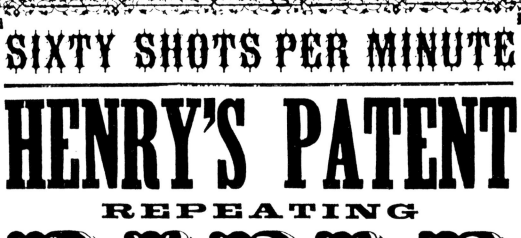

SIXTY SHOTS PER MINUTE

HENRY'S PATENT

REPEATING

RIFLE

The Most Effective Weapon in the World.

This Rifle can be discharged 16 times without loading or taking down from the shoulder, or even loosing aim. It is also slung in such a manner, that either on horse or on foot, it can be **Instantly Used**, without taking the strap from the shoulder.

For a House or Sporting Arm, it has no Equal;

IT IS ALWAYS LOADED AND ALWAYS READY.

The size now made is 44-100 inch bore, 24 inch barrel, and carries a conical ball 32 to the pound. The penetration at 100 yards is 8 inches; at 400 yards 5 inches; and it carries with force sufficient to kill at 1,000 yards.

A resolute man, armed with one of these Rifles, particularly if on horseback, CANNOT BE CAPTURED.

" We particularly commend it for ARMY USES, as the most effective arm for picket and vidette duty, and to all our citizens in secluded places, as a protection against guerilla attacks and robberies. A man armed with one of these Rifles, can load and discharge one shot every second, so that he is equal to a company every minute, a regiment every ten minutes, a brigade every half hour, and a division every hour."—*Louisville Journal.*

Address JNO. W. BROWN,

Gen'l Ag't, Columbus, Ohio,

At Rail Road Building, near the Depot.

Above: Bold claims made in the advertising flier of Midwest agent John W. Brown. Some Midwestern military units purchased Henry rifles in the Civil War.

it at my own table in the presence of my family." The guerrillas agreed to let the captain go outside to be shot, but he dove into a log crib where he had hidden his Henry rifle, and in the subsequent firefight killed all of the seven attackers. The Kentucky authorities, so the story went, then purchased Henrys for Wilson's entire company.

Winchester carried on an intensive advertising program through his network of dealers, especially in the Middle West. His advertising flier claimed it as "The Most Effective Weapon In The World, Sixty Shots Per Minute." Describing the rifle as "having no equal as a house or sporting arm," the

broadside concludes, "... a resolute man, armed with one of these Rifles, particularly on horseback, Cannot Be Captured."

Many more orders were received than could be met, indicating that if the Ordnance Department had supported the new invention additional contractors would have been engaged to produce the new rifle, as was the case with the Springfield rifle musket, which was produced by some 20 private contractors as well as the Springfield Armory. Colonel J. T. Wilder of the First Brigade Fifth Division, 14th Army Corps, in Murfreesboro, Tennessee, wrote to Winchester on March 20, 1863, asking for a price for 900 rifles, which his men indicated they would purchase. As it turned out, since Winchester could not produce this many, the brigade settled for Spencer carbines.

The only regiment of the Army of the Potomac which was equipped with Henry rifles was Colonel Lafayette C. Baker's

Above: An early engraving of Confederate Civil War troops attacking Union forces at Allatoona Pass; the Federals repelled the attack with Henry rifles (not shown).

First Washington, D.C., Cavalry. Its duties were primarily to guard the District of Columbia, but in May, 1863, the regiment was attached to General Kautz's cavalry division in a raid on Petersburg, Virginia. The colonel's memoirs relate how a body of Rebel troops on its way to Petersburg was routed in amazingly short order, and 60 prisoners were taken.

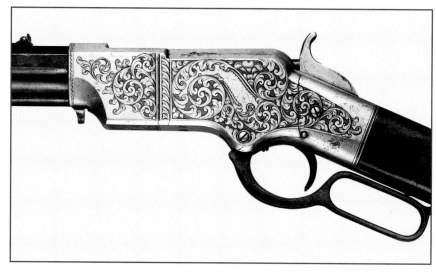

Right: Silver plated Henry rifle engraved by Louis D. Nimschke. The sculptural scrollwork and punched dot background are typical of Nimschke engraving.

One of the prisoners said, "... the Northerners must have had a whole army, from the way the bullets flew." Later a Confederate breastwork was attacked by dismounted troopers firing their Henrys steadily as they advanced. When the position was taken in this early example of assault by storm, it was found the Union troops had been outnumbered three to one.

A set of letters accompanying a Henry rifle marked with the name of a soldier of the 7th Illinois Volunteer Infantry, now in the possession of a member of the American Society of Arms Collectors, echoes similar results. In July 1864, the members of the regiment had all bought Henrys at a cost of $41, equal to three month's Army pay. In October of that year, the regiment took part in the Battle of Allatoona Pass, Georgia, a railroad depot playing an important role in the supply of General William Sherman's forces advancing on Atlanta. The Federal troops, outnumbered three to two, held off several Confederate attacks. About 5,500 soldiers were engaged and over 1,600 were killed or wounded, making the casualty rate second only to Gettysburg. It was the increased firepower provided by the Henry rifles that made the difference.

The Henry on the Frontier

While the Civil War slowed Western migration and produced a lull in clashes with the Native Americans, the Henry rifle grew in popularity on the frontier. An incident late in 1865 was one of the earliest experiences that the Native Americans of the Rocky Mountains area had of the deadly effect of a repeating firearm. Two white former Union soldiers who had kept their Henry rifles began mining borax in the heart of the Blackfoot Indian country of Montana. One morning they saw some forty Blackfoot warriors approach, dismount nearly at gun range, and begin creeping toward them. The miners anticipated the usual Indian tactic of exposing themselves briefly to draw fire and then charging before the defenders would have time to reload. The miners fired their two usual opening shots, and then, as the

Blackfeet rushed at them, began a continuous fire from their Henrys. Only a few of the attackers escaped unhit, and after that the miners' camp was shunned by the Native Americans. Later, one of the surviving attackers was quoted as telling of the "Spirit Guns."

Another famous story of the Henry rifle in the West is about Steve Venard, marshal of Nevada City, the California mining town. A stagecoach carrying a large amount of cash was robbed near the town by three armed bandits at 4:30 a.m. on a May morning in 1866. Later that morning Venard picked up the robbers' trail and killed all three with his Henry rifle in successive confrontations, and also recovered the cash. The governor of California made Venard a lieutenant colonel of militia, and the express company gave him a $3,000 reward plus an inscribed new Henry.

Today the Henry rifle has a surprisingly modern look, together with a most attractive sculptural quality. It is a fitting predecessor to the tremendous popularity of Winchester's succeeding models.

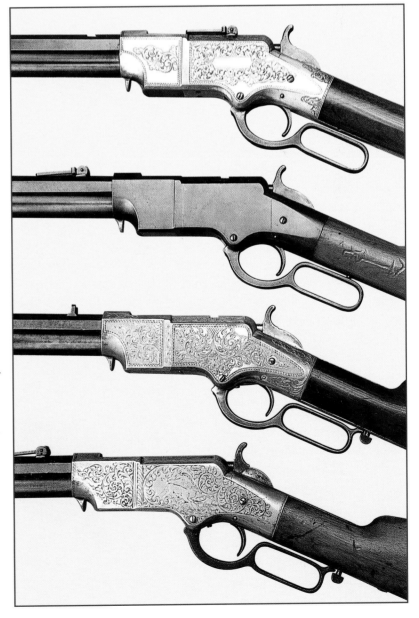

Right: From the top, Henry rifle, serial number 11, factory engraved; iron frame Henry, serial number 73, in outstanding condition; factory engraved Henry with gold-plated frame and rosewood stock; and Henry with Nimschke engraving.

"THE GUNS THAT WON THE WEST"
MODELS 1866, 1873, AND 1876

The Model 1866

The Winchester Repeating Arms Company, with Oliver Winchester and his family owning more than half the stock, initiated plans immediately after the end of the Civil War in 1865 to move its operations to larger quarters in Bridgeport, Connecticut. This was carried out in 1866, and the company also brought in Nelson King as the new superintendent. Just as B. Tyler Henry had been hired in 1858 with instructions to upgrade the Volcanic rifle to the Henry rifle, King was instructed to improve the Henry. He did this very effectively, with the patent issued under his name in March, 1866. In his book, *Winchester Repeating Arms Company*, Herbert G. Houze reports evidence that the first production of the improved rifle took place in August 1866. It was christened in the West as the "Yellow Boy," and it is interesting to note that Winchester considered bringing out the new rifle with an iron instead of a brass frame, but decided against doing that because of the stock of already existing tools and fixtures for brass frames left over from the Henry.

There is little personal information about King, but he must have been extraordinarily competent, since he stayed on as superintendent until approximately 1875. His improvements were considered so important that the company's board of directors voted him a bonus of $5,000, which he took mostly in company stock, and his salary was the highest in the company except for that of the president, Oliver Winchester.

Yearly production figures shown in *The Winchester Book* by George Madis indicate that production of the Henry and the Model 1866 continued through the year 1866 at the level of the Civil War years, with the Model 1866 production falling off in 1867, probably affected by the move to Bridgeport. Then, starting in 1868, it exceeded the Civil War level, and by 1871 reached a peak of eight times the annual Civil War number. These

figures are reflected in the growth of employment in the company: this reached 260 in 1869 in Bridgeport, compared with the Civil War peak of 101 in New Haven in 1864.

It is not clear from the production data by serial numbers whether military sales to foreign countries are included. It appears that they are not, since the amount of reported overseas sales is considerably higher. Houze concludes, in fact, that contrary to other writers' views there is no overlapping between the serial numbers of the Henry rifle and the Model 1866, meaning that the Model 1866 started with the serial number 1.

In any event, Oliver Winchester, undeterred by the lack of interest by the U.S. military, was convinced of this rifle's advantages for military use, and did succeed in obtaining substantial overseas orders. The musket versions were fitted with a bayonet lug designed for military use. In his 1865 European vacation trip, Winchester submitted his Henry rifle to the Swiss Government for trials in a competition with other arms and it took first

Above: Winchester plant superintendent Nelson King, who developed King's Improvement, a loading gate on the side of the frame, converting the Henry rifle to the highly successful Model 1866 "Yellow Boy."

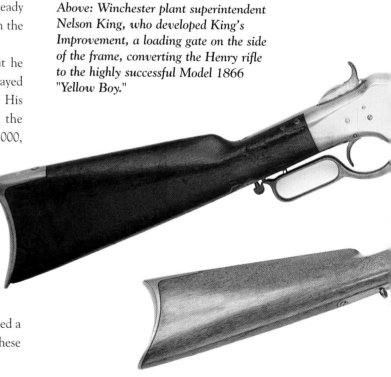

Right: Thomas E. Addis, Winchester supersalesman who produced huge overseas orders for Winchester rifles and ammunition. He sold rifles to the Mexicans who overthrew Maximilian.

place, although the Swiss ended up buying only a small amount of machinery rather than rifles.

The first of a series of foreign orders which apparently comprised most of Winchester's business between 1866 and 1876 was obtained by Thomas Emmett Addis, described by George Madis in *The Winchester Book* as one of the most famous men associated with Winchester. He had started with the company as a workman in the primer department, and worked his way up by 1866 to become the chief foreign sales representative, "with unlimited territory and unlimited authority to conduct any of the company's business necessary to make sales." That year he went to Mexico, where the French had installed Maximilian as Emperor of Mexico. Benito Juarez was attempting to win back the country for the Republic, and ordered 1,000 Winchester rifles with 500 cartridges for each gun. There is a colorful story of how Addis managed to deliver the arms from Brownsville, Texas, to Monterrey. After obtaining payment of $57,000 in silver from the *Juaristas* by threatening to turn the guns over to Maximilian, he made his way back to Brownsville through bandit-infested territory, staying awake at night on a three day trip by sticking himself with his scarf pin. Addis (born O'Connor, and changing his name to honor a supposed Irish hero) stayed on the road for Winchester until his retirement in 1901 and had the following lettered on his tombstone: "In Memory of Thomas Emmett Addis – Traveler."

Sources of overseas orders included Chile, Peru, and the French Government, which ordered 3,000 muskets and 3,000 carbines at the outbreak of the Franco-Prussian War. The largest order came from Turkey, in 1870, for 46,000 muskets and 5,000 carbines, plus ammunition. The Turks provided additional profitable orders not long afterward.

Oliver Winchester went to Constantinople (Istanbul) and brought back an order for 200,000 Martini-Henry rifles, which he sold to the Providence Tool Company in Rhode Island. That company had produced the predecessor to that rifle, which the British Army adopted. (Martini was a Swiss inventor and Alexander Henry, no relation to B. Tyler Henry, was a Scottish gunsmith, and the gun had no relation to the Henry rifle produced by Winchester). The Turks also placed a huge order with Winchester for ammunition for Martini-Henry and British Snider cartridges. The purchases were timely in that Russia declared war on Turkey in 1877, ending

Above: Model 1866 Yellow Boy with brass receiver. This saddle carbine was captured by the British during the Boer War, 1899-1902.

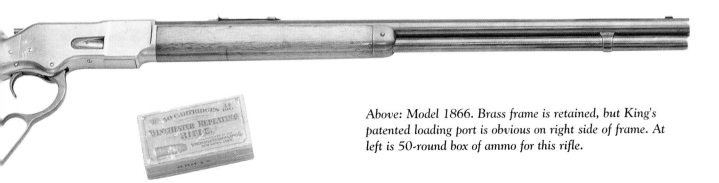

Above: Model 1866. Brass frame is retained, but King's patented loading port is obvious on right side of frame. At left is 50-round box of ammo for this rifle.

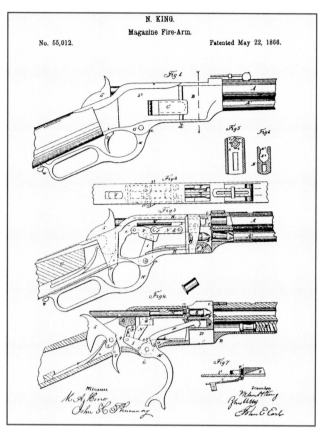

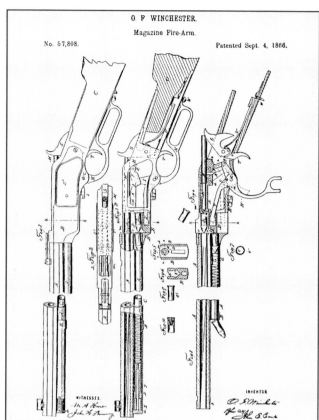

Above: Patent drawing of the Model 1866 rifle with King's Improvement. Before this improvement, with the Henry rifle, the cartridges had to be loaded from the front of the magazine.

Above: Further patent drawing, for the Model 1866, this time under the name of Oliver F. Winchester. The highly valued Nelson King stayed with the company until his retirement in 1875.

in 1878 with Turkey's acceptance of an independent Bulgaria.

A famous story about the Winchester rifles in Turkey is quoted in R. L. Wilson's *Winchester, An American Legend*, attributed to Rear Admiral Jasper Selwyn of the British Navy in 1882:

"I have been for a long time a consistent advocate of the magazine gun known as the Winchester, or the Winchester-Henry as it is also called . . . I saw personally in Turkey during the [Russo-Turkish War of 1877] the Circassian cavalry all armed with the Winchester-Henry [1866] carbine. My friend Reouf Pasha . . . told me he was reconnoitering at Yeni Zahrah with only his personal bodyguard of some thirty Circassians. A Cossack regiment, some 600 strong, came down and surrounded him. It was toward nightfall; he got his Circassian guard off their horses and made them all lie down, they and their horses. He said to them: 'Now, my children, we are in a mess, and must sell ourselves dearly to the Ruski.' The Cossacks formed around them, thinking they had only to prevent their escape, but in five minutes so many of the Cossacks were killed, not one of the Circassians being touched, that the Cossacks decided

to leave them alone and to go away. That shows the value of magazine weapons."

The success of the Model 1866 gave Winchester the opportunity to start a long continued process of absorbing other companies which might compete in the repeating arms field. A major success was the acquisition of the Spencer Repeating Rifle Company of Boston, in 1868. The Spencer rifle and carbine had won out over the Henry rifle for U.S. military purchases during the Civil War, and found some continued use after the war by the U.S. Cavalry and frontier settlers. However, the lack of military business hurt the Spencer Company after the war, and founder Christopher Spencer left to try, unsuccessfully, to develop other repeating rifles.

A second company acquired by Winchester was the American Repeating Rifle Company, formerly the Fogarty Arms Company, of Boston, which had several patents for improvements which could have competed with Winchester. A third was the Adirondack Arms Company of Plattsburgh, New York, in 1874, which had developed a rifle with a modified bolt action and a tubular magazine under the barrel.

The company was in such a firm financial position that between 1870 and 1871 it was able to buy land and construct a new, larger factory in New Haven, leaving its rented quarters in Bridgeport. The site, at Munson Street and Canal Street (later changed to Winchester Avenue), was bought from Winchester himself, whose palatial home was nearby on Prospect Street. This is still an avenue of fine homes and institutional buildings, many connected with Yale University, extending north along the top of a ridge from the center of New Haven. The factory site is in the valley immediately to the west, and it appears to be a tribute to Oliver Winchester's foresight that the land was available for the ultimate expansion of the plant in 1916 to 81 acres with over 3 million feet of building floor space, and 17,500 employees. As explained later, the present modern Winchester plant, with 300 employees, is located on part of this original site, producing through modern technology as many rifle barrels as did the original huge plant.

Members of Oliver Winchester's family came to the fore during this period. His son William Wirt Winchester became vice president in 1871, and Thomas Gray Bennett, who married William Wirt's younger sister, became Secretary. The company's stockholders were so happy that they adopted the following resolution on April 4, 1871, after which they increased Oliver Winchester's salary from $5,000 to $10,000:

"*Whereas:* O. F. Winchester, President and Founder of the company has for fifteen years displayed the most untiring perseverance and under every discouraging circumstance imaginable, by consummate financial skill and inventive genius has succeeded in perfecting the most perfect arm in the world, which the last war in Europe has so favorably tested, and the very handsome returns to the stockholders enables us fully to appreciate, therefore

Resolved that the thanks of the stockholders are most heartily tendered Mr. Winchester with the hope that he may live long to enjoy the fruits of his well earned success."

Below: Thomas Gray Bennett, husband of Oliver Winchester's daughter and who became the longtime company president, with son Winchester Bennett and grandson T. G. Bennett.

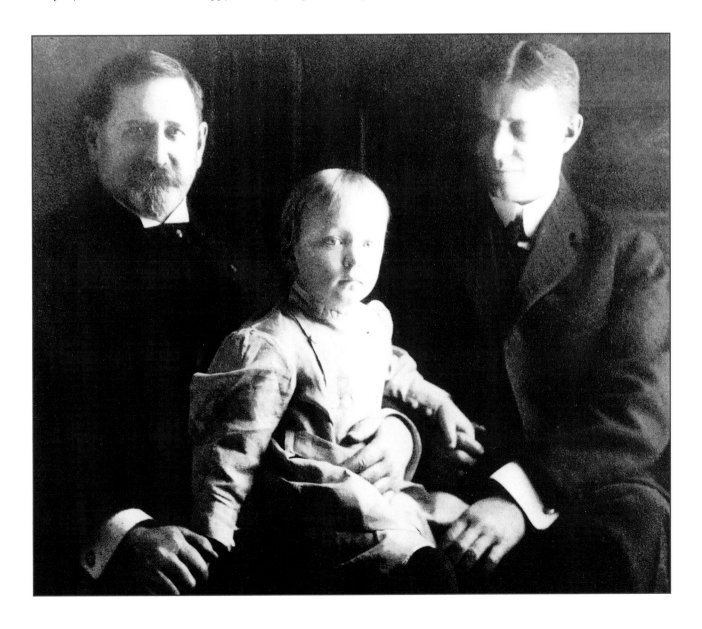

While from 1866 to 1873 military sales overseas comprised most of Winchester's business, a third or more of the output was for domestic sales, through a network of some 19 jobbers and dealers. Some familiar names for collectors include Schuyler, Hartley and Graham of New York, E. K. Tryon of Philadelphia, Freund and Brother of Cheyenne, Wyoming, and William Golcher of San Francisco. The "Yellow Boy" was well known on the Western frontier.

While settlers including Civil War veterans were increasingly moving West, the only protection from clashes with the Native Americans, whose ancestral lands were being invaded and whose means of livelihood such as the buffalo were being eliminated, was a string of forts maintained by only 20,000 Army troops. There had been previous clashes during the Civil War, including major raids and reprisals in Minnesota and Colonel Chivington's massacre of Black Kettle's village at Sand Creek in Colorado. Now there were some 50,000 of the total of some 200,000 Native Americans in the West who were overtly hostile.

The soldiers were armed only with weapons left over from the Civil War, such as the Spencer carbine, but the Native Americans saw the advantages of the Winchester rifle and captured them from settlers and cowboys whenever they could. Under government regulations, white traders were supposed to sell only obsolete muzzleloaders, but some Winchesters fell into Native American hands through these traders. A number of Winchesters, both Henrys and the Model 1866, have been found with patterns of brass tacks on their stocks, a sign of Native American usage. There was no way for the natives to make ammunition, but they sometimes showed ingenuity in converting the rifles to muzzleloaders with loose powder and ball.

The period after the Civil War also saw the beginning of the great cattle drives from Texas first to Kansas, and then further West as the railroads advanced. The tradition of the cowboy began with the Mexican vaqueros or "cow-hunters," men who gathered the wild longhorns left over from the Spanish days into herds for ranches. The cowboys were not as romantic as pictured in movies, but were an independent breed. One out of three were Mexicans or blacks. By 1871 they were driving as many as 600,000 to 700,000 cattle per year northward. As related by William C. Davis in *The American Frontier*, every 2,000 to 3,000 cattle required from eight to twenty cowboys to manage them on the drive, along with a cook, a wrangler to take care of the cowboys' horses, and perhaps a foreman. A Henry or Model 1866 rifle would clearly have great advantages for hunting game and for self defense, but would have been relatively expensive for the average cowboy. A Winchester cost around $40; the standard cowboy pay was $30 per month.

This period in the West also gave rise to the legend of the outlaw and the gunfighter. There was certainly a lawless

continued on page 36

Model 1866

Type: 14-shot carbine; 18-shot rifles and muskets.

Made: 1866-1891.

Variations: First model, serial range 12476 to approximately 15550; only carbines and rifles; main feature the "Henry drop" in the profile of the frame ahead of the hammer. Second model, serial range to approximately 23000; "Henry drop" reduced and the frame flared to meet the forearm; muskets produced as well as rifles and carbines. Third model, serial range to 149000, curved frame profile less pronounced; rifles, carbines, and muskets produced. Fourth model, serial range to approximately 170101; still less curve in frame profile; rifles, carbines and muskets produced.

Quantity: Total approximately 157,000, including 118,000 carbines, 6,000 rifles, and 13,000 muskets.

Caliber: .44 rimfire.

Barrel length: Carbine 20 inches, rifle 24 inches, musket 27 inches.

Markings: On barrel, to serial number approximately 23000, HENRY'S PATENT OCT. 16, 1860, KING'S PATENT, MARCH 29, 1866; for succeeding serial numbers, WINCHESTER'S REPEATING ARMS, NEW HAVEN, CT., KING'S IMPROVEMENT PATENTED MARCH 29, 1866, OCTOBER 16, 1860. Finish same as the Henry. Engraving was provided by special order.

Mechanical function: Among changes from the Henry rifle, the bolt assembly was modified to protect the extractor spring. A wooden forearm was added under the barrel in front of the receiver, extending part way down the length of the barrel. Most importantly, the tubular magazine under the barrel was completely enclosed, instead of having an open slot as in the Henry, a loading gate was added to the side of the receiver, and loading was changed from the front of the magazine to the rear. A mechanism was provided in which each cartridge inserted would push those already in the magazine forward, up to the limit of the magazine's capacity. The loading gate with a spring such that it closed after each cartridge was inserted. Weight substantially less since magazine was a lightweight tube instead of being machined integral with the barrel. Safety half cock on hammer.

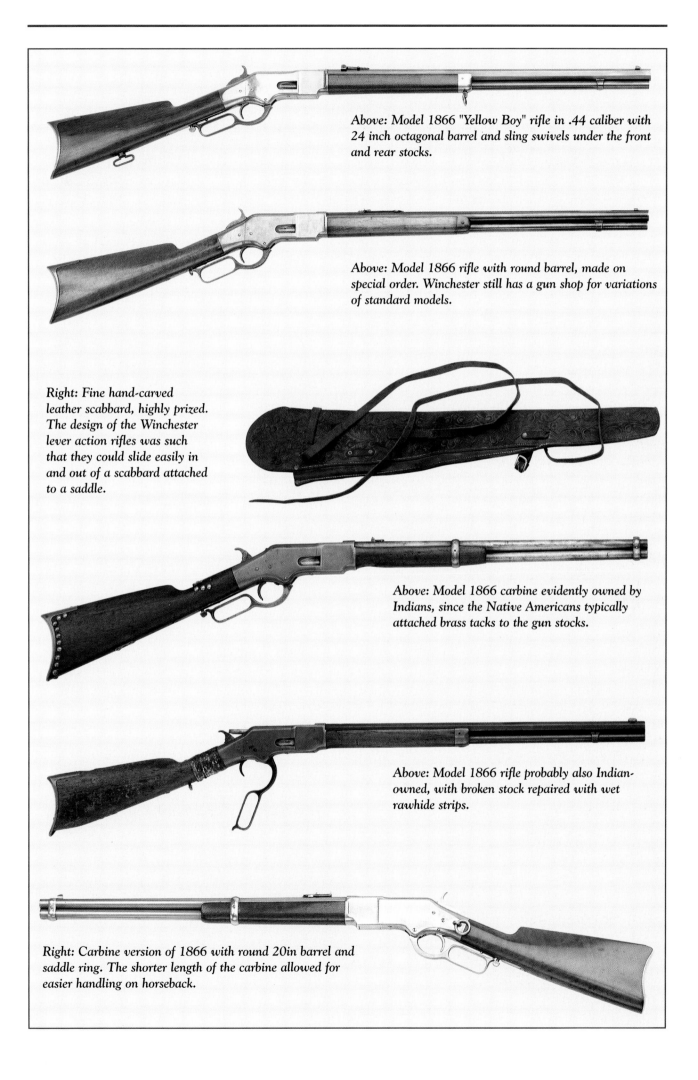

Above: Model 1866 "Yellow Boy" rifle in .44 caliber with 24 inch octagonal barrel and sling swivels under the front and rear stocks.

Above: Model 1866 rifle with round barrel, made on special order. Winchester still has a gun shop for variations of standard models.

Right: Fine hand-carved leather scabbard, highly prized. The design of the Winchester lever action rifles was such that they could slide easily in and out of a scabbard attached to a saddle.

Above: Model 1866 carbine evidently owned by Indians, since the Native Americans typically attached brass tacks to the gun stocks.

Above: Model 1866 rifle probably also Indian-owned, with broken stock repaired with wet rawhide strips.

Right: Carbine version of 1866 with round 20in barrel and saddle ring. The shorter length of the carbine allowed for easier handling on horseback.

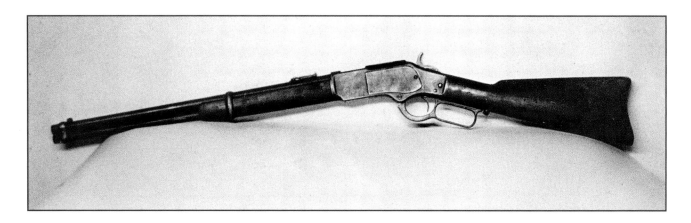

element that moved West after the Civil War, such as Jesse James and his brother, Frank, who had ridden with the bloody Confederate guerrilla Quantrill during the war. Also, the burgeoning cattle towns like Abilene, Kansas, at first had no organized force of lawmen. "Wild Bill" Hickok was engaged as marshal in Abilene in 1871 after serving as an Army scout and killing three men as sheriff in two other Kansas towns. He spent most of his time gambling, and was sacked in Abilene after a shootout outside a saloon in which he mistakenly killed one of his own deputies. He was shot in the back and killed in 1876 in Deadwood Gulch in South Dakota while holding what became the "dead man's hand" in a card game.

Whether or not the Winchester "Won the West," it was a popular and valuable tool for the growing population on the Western frontier.

The Model 1873

This is the best known of all the Winchester arms, although its long period of production, from 1873 to 1923, takes many of these rifles out of the period of the "Western frontier." According to George Madis in *The Winchester Book*, the year 1890 is generally agreed to mark the end of the frontier, which is defined as a region with more than two and less than six people per square mile; an area with lower population than that is regarded as a wilderness.

The major advance represented by the Model 1873, besides its stronger and lighter steel frame, was its use of the more powerful centerfire cartridge. The nomenclature of the .44-40, the size which came out first and was the primary

Above: Jesse James's Model 1866 Winchester carbine. His raids on trains and banks evidently required the lighter version of the Model 1866

Right: Geologist John F. Steward with his Model 1866 Winchester rifle, standing in Glen Canyon of the Colorado River in 1871.

caliber used for the Model 1873, refers to its .44 caliber and charge of 40 grains of black powder. This compared with only 28 grains of powder used in the rimfire cartridge for the Henry and Model 1866. A larger load cannot be used in a rimfire cartridge because the metal must be thin enough to be indented by the firing pin, making the case to weak for heavy loads. The centerfire cartridge was more difficult to develop and manufacture, which accounts for Winchester not being able to use it for volume production until 1874.

The year 1873 also saw the introduction of the Colt Single Action Army or Peacemaker revolver. Although this famous handgun was adopted by the U.S. Army in .45 caliber, Colt's lost no time in offering the revolver to the civilian market in all three of the calibers adopted for the Winchester rifle. An advantage was that the user, with the same cartridge, could carry both his Colt revolver in a holster on his hip and his Winchester rifle in saddle scabbard. This became the icon of the knight of the Western plains,

Above: Another view of the Indian-decorated Model 1866 Winchester carbine shown on page 35. Most Indian-owned carbines are not found in as good condition as this one.

immortalized in countless Western movies and an image which undoubtedly has contributed to the success of Winchester lever action arms over the years. Even now, in comparison with the modern high power bolt action hunting rifle, the lever action arm fits better in a saddle scabbard, having no protuberances on the side.

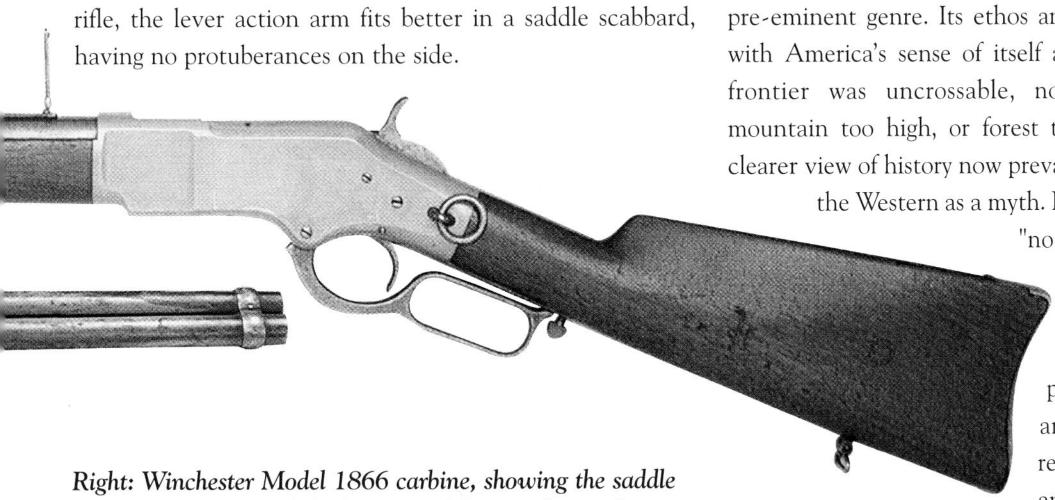

Right: Winchester Model 1866 carbine, showing the saddle ring on the left side of the frame, and front and rear sling swivels. The saddle ring was included on most makes of civilian and military carbines through the 1800s.

A recent commentary in the *New York Times*, "Sending Out a Search Party for the Western," explores why few movies of this type are currently being made. As stated by the article, "It was not long ago that the Western was America's pre-eminent genre. Its ethos and its codes were bound up with America's sense of itself as the nation for which no frontier was uncrossable, no enemy untameable, no mountain too high, or forest too dense for conquest." A clearer view of history now prevails, showing some aspects of the Western as a myth. However, the article goes on, "nothing has emerged to replicate the Western's heady blend of action, excitement, romance and poetry." It is significant, the article indicates, that as recently as 1995, John Wayne and Clint Eastwood were first and second in a poll of the country's most popular movie stars, even though Wayne had been dead for 16 years.

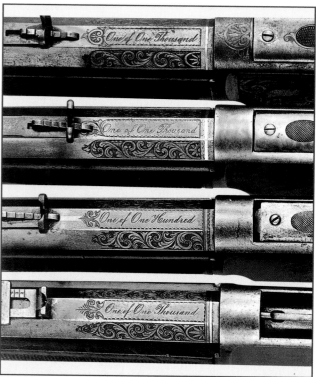

Above: The young and handsome John Wayne as he appeared in the movie "Stagecoach," holding a Winchester rifle at the ready (anachronistically a Model 1892 instead of a Model 1873).

Above: Three "One of One Thousand" Winchester Model 1873 rifles, and an even scarcer "One of One Hundred." The script and engraving are standardized. There is some variation in the sliding dust covers at the right.

It is the Model 1873 Winchester, along with the Colt Peacemaker, that is indelibly associated with the concept, however cinematic, of the "Winning of the West." John Wayne carried a Winchester (a later version, the 1892) in his earliest starring movie, "Stagecoach," was probably at his most romantic in "Hondo," and still charged the bad men on horseback, twirling a Winchester with an oversized finger loop, as a retired lawman in "True Grit." There is a splendid larger-than-life sized statue of Wayne carrying his Winchester at the entrance to the current Winchester factory in New Haven, with additional copies at the Wayne mansion in California and at the Buffalo Bill Historical Center in Cody, Wyoming.

There was even a Western movie in which the Winchester was the star, "Winchester '73," which appeared in 1950. The story was about a rare variation of the Model 1873 which was brought out by Winchester starting in 1875 as a marketing device. Of all the rifle barrels tested when they came off the production line, the most accurate of each 1,000 was made into a rifle with extra finish including set triggers, and engraved on the top of the barrel "One of One

Thousand" or "One of 1000." At the time, these were sold for the princely sum of $100 (now equivalent to about $15,000.) Somewhat fewer were made with barrels not quite as fine, marked "One of One Hundred".

In the movie, which stars James Stewart and Stephen McNally, Stewart's Western character wins a One of 1000 rifle in a shooting match, the envious outlaw McNally steals it, and Stewart retrieves it in the final showdown. Interestingly, according to R .L. Wilson's *Winchester, The Golden Age of American Gunmaking and the Winchester One of 1000*, the script is believed to have been based on the story of an actual lawman, Henry N. Brown, who was presented with a finely engraved and inscribed Model 1873 rifle by the citizens of Caldwell, Kansas, in December of 1882. A year later, Brown turned outlaw, and was captured robbing a bank in neighboring Medicine Lodge. He and three accomplices were killed by a lynch mob the same night. Brown wrote a letter to his wife from his jail cell, apologizing for his actions and urging her to sell all his things, "but keep the Winchester." The rifle is now at the Kansas State Historical Society in Topeka.

continued on page 42

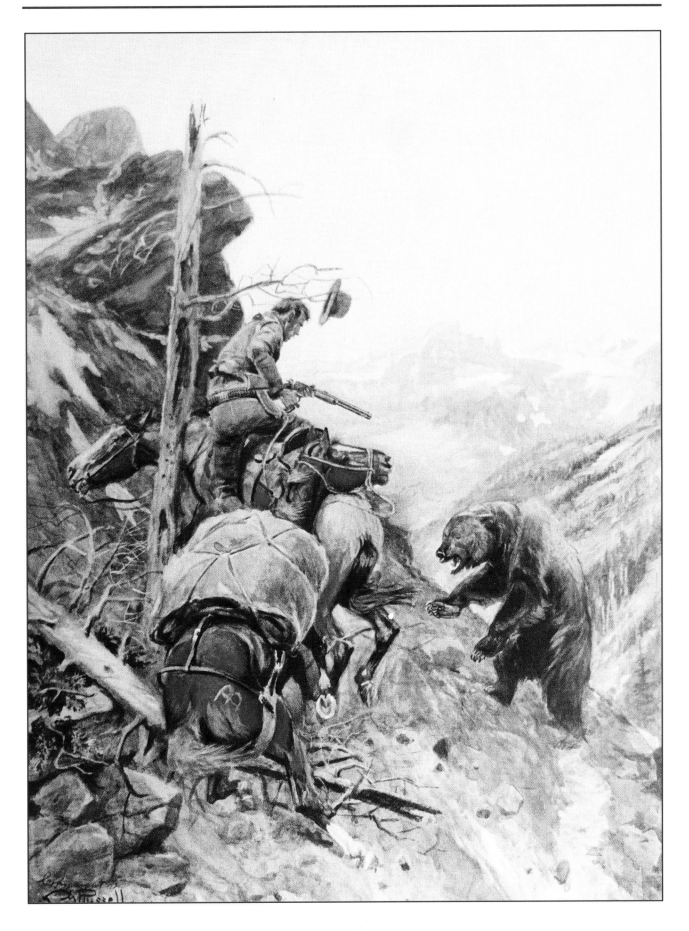

Left: Model 1873 in .44-40, bought in Texas and probably used for hunting buffalo by railroad locating engineer, shown with standard rifle scabbard (reproduced at different proportion) of about 1880, purchased for use with this rifle.

Above: Splendid 1908 action painting by Charles M. Russell, A Disputed Trail, featuring a Winchester lever action rifle. Ironically, Russell considered himself only an illustrator, not a painter!

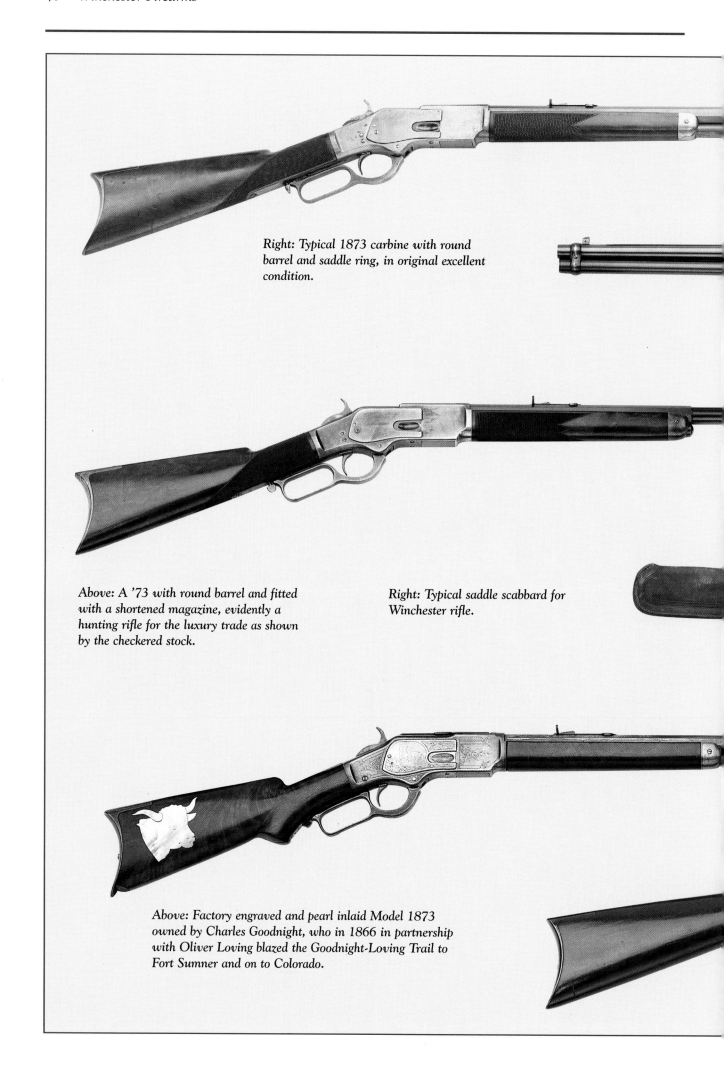

Right: Typical 1873 carbine with round barrel and saddle ring, in original excellent condition.

Above: A '73 with round barrel and fitted with a shortened magazine, evidently a hunting rifle for the luxury trade as shown by the checkered stock.

Right: Typical saddle scabbard for Winchester rifle.

Above: Factory engraved and pearl inlaid Model 1873 owned by Charles Goodnight, who in 1866 in partnership with Oliver Loving blazed the Goodnight-Loving Trail to Fort Sumner and on to Colorado.

Left: Model 1873 rifle with standard octagonal barrel and with extra finish including nickel plating and checkered burl walnut stock.

Above: Model 1873 rifle with shortened barrel to serve as carbine.

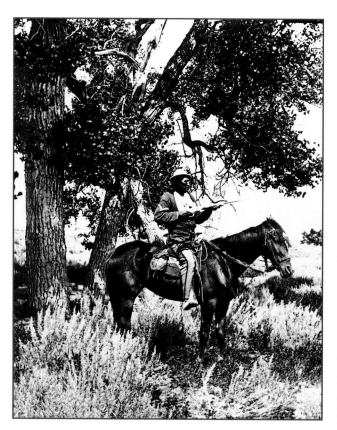

Above: Bloody Knife, Custer's scout, on Yellowstone Expedition, photographed 1873. The rifle appears to be a Winchester Model 1873 with a shortened magazine.

The One of 1000 and One of 100 rifles are now great rarities on the collectors' market. Only 136 of the former and 8 of the latter were made. When the "Winchester '73" movie was released, a search was advertised for surviving rifles, and since that time as many as 61 One of 1000s have been located in Model 1873 and six more in Model 1876. Only six of the scarcer One of 100s have been identified. The One of 1000s are currently valued on the collectors' market at up to $125,000.

While, beginning in 1873, Winchester's overseas military business such as in Turkey fell off, there were apparently large sales of 1873 muskets to the Chinese Government. The company embarked on a major expansion of its already large ammunition business, intending to supply the market with all types. This brought the company into direct competition with the largest firm in

Right: The Winchester Model 1873 awarded to Henry Brown while marshal of Medicine Lodge, Kansas, before he became an outlaw for the second time (see photo on page 10). Now at the Kansas State Historical Society, Topeka.

the industry, the Union Metallic Cartridge Company, headed by Marcellus Hartley. He was associated also with the famous New York dealer Schuyler Hartley and Graham, and also later became president of the Remington Company, a major arms producer. However, Winchester and Hartley made an agreement not to contest each other's patents on ammunition. The ammunition business lent itself to large companies even more than did arms production, because large investments were needed in equipment rather than manpower. Also, the manufacture of gunpowder became increasingly specialized, contributing to the growth of the Olin Corporation which later acquired Winchester and still manufactures the Winchester ammunition. This part of its business was always important for Winchester, for example accounting for 50 percent of its sales in 1888.

It is ironic, and a further commentary on how difficult it is to move the U.S. Army into new developments, that 1873 also saw the complete rejection by the Army of the repeating rifle. With the end of the Civil War in 1865 the Army was left with large stocks of Model 1861 type muskets and Spencer and Sharps carbines. Some Spencers were still used for the cavalry, but were largely obsolete. A number of Sharps carbines were converted to .50-70 centerfire cartridges, and many Springfield rifle muskets or their parts were adapted to the new single-shot .50-70 musket. In 1873 the Army settled on the .45-70 cartridge and had the Springfield Armory produce new single-shot rifle muskets and carbines. The latter became the standard rifle used by the cavalry.

The adequacy of the Springfield carbine became a serious issue at the Battle of the Little Bighorn on June 25, 1876, when Lieutenant Colonel (Civil War Brevet General) George Armstrong Custer and 215 Seventh Cavalry troopers were surrounded and killed to a man by some 2,000 Sioux warriors, some using Winchester rifles. It is tempting to

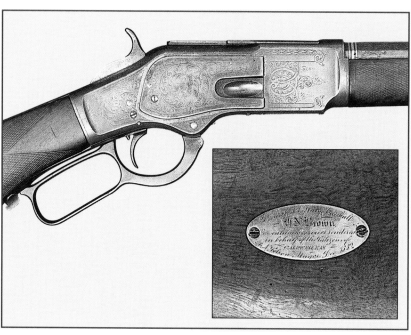

speculate whether the fight would have turned out differently if the troopers had been armed themselves with Winchesters. It seems that the rifle's rapid firing capability of 15 shots in the magazine plus one shot in the chamber without reloading would have made up for the ten to one advantage in numbers held by the Sioux. The troopers' Springfield carbines, in addition to having to be reloaded after each shot, had problems with extracting the cartridges.

Above: "Double W" cartridge board, c. 1897. Scene in center is an A. B. Frost print honoring B. Tyler Henry.

Also, their spare ammunition was held on the troopers' horses, which the Sioux dispersed. It can of course be argued that Custer should not have been so foolhardy in dividing his regiment and in not scouting ahead to see how many Sioux were present.

MODEL 1873

Type: 15-shot lever action rifle; 12-shot carbine; 17-shot musket. Also, six-shot sporting rifle with short magazine, short barrel carbine known as the Trapper's Model, and, from 1885 to 1904, rifle in .22 caliber.

Made: 1873-1919 (additional rifles assembled from parts in inventory to 1924).

Variations: In the configuration of the dust cover, trigger pin, and lever latch. Early first model to serial approximately 1600; late first model to serial 31000. Second model to serial 90000. Third model, serial above 90000 starting 1882. Also "One of 1,000" special model, 136 made, and "One of 100", 8 made.

Quantity: 720,610, including 19,552 made in .22 caliber.

Caliber: .44-40, .38-40 starting 1879, and .32-20 starting in

1882, all centerfire; plus .22 rimfire, short and long.

Barrel length: Rifle 24$\frac{1}{2}$ inches, carbine 20 inches, musket 30 inches, with some 26 and 27 inches. Trapper Model, 14 to 18 inch barrels.

Markings: On barrel, WINCHESTER'S REPEATING ARMS, NEW HAVEN, CONN. U.S.A. KING'S IMPROVEMENT PATENTED MARCH 29, 1866. OCTOBER 16, 1860. Most with caliber markings on barrel or underneath on carrier block. Barrel blued, receiver casehardened iron (earliest production) or steel. Engraving on special order.

Mechanical function: Lever action, similar to the Henry and Model 1866. Central firing pin. Wood forearm. A sliding dust cover was added to protect the mechanism inside the receiver.

Left: 1886 photo of Geronimo (far right), holding .45-70 trapdoor Springfield, with his brother-in-law Yanozha, (far left, holding 1873 Winchester carbine), son Chappo (with another 1873 carbine), and second cousin Fun (with .45-70 Springfield carbine).

Below: Texas Rangers, Frontier Battalion, Company D, 1885. All are armed with the Winchester Model 1873, evidently ready for use.

In any event, even though the Army was under pressure to find a better rifle after the massacre, the lever action Winchester continued to be ignored and it was only in 1892 that the Springfield single-shot rifle was given up, and even then for the Krag bolt action in .30-40 caliber. The Krag range of rifles were developed by Norwegians Colonel Ole Krag, director of the Køngsberg Arsenal, with the help of Eric Jorgensen, the works superintendant, and were known also as the Krag-Jorgensens.) In Germany, the modern bolt action Mauser rifle was developed as early as 1888. Ironically, the Army did purchase 10,000 lever action Model 1895 Winchester Muskets for use in the Spanish-American War of 1898, for which they arrived too late. By that time, bolt action rifles were standard for modern armies.

Many testimonials came in from the West for the Model 1873 Winchester, such as the following from Colonel William F. "Buffalo Bill" Cody, which was featured in Winchester's 1875 catalog:

"I have been using and have thoroughly tested your latest improved rifle. Allow me to say that I have tried and used nearly every kind of gun made in the United States, and for general hunting, or Indian fighting, I pronounce your improved Winchester the boss.

An Indian will give more for one of your guns than any other gun he can get.

While in the Black Hills this last summer I crippled a bear, and Mr. Bear made for me, and I am certain had I not been armed with one of your repeating rifles I would now be in the happy hunting grounds. The bear was not thirty feet from me when he charged, but before he could reach me I (put) more lead (in him) than he could comfortably digest.

Believe me, that you have the *most complete* rifle now made."

Buffalo Bill's traveling Wild West Show, which he started in 1883 and continued until 1916, provided great publicity for Winchester rifles. The show included fancy shooting, including of Winchesters; a buffalo hunt; the capture of the Deadwood (South Dakota) stagecoach; a Pony Express ride; hard-riding cowboys; and yelling Native Americans. Annie Oakley, known as "Little Sure Shot," was one of the stars.

Buffalo Bill was an authentic hero of the Western frontier. As a teenager he rode for the Pony Express from 1860 to 1861, which covered the distance from the Missouri River to the Pacific coast in 10 days. He served in the Civil War. After that, as a civilian scout for the Army, he took part in 16 fights with the Native Americans and was awarded the Medal of Honor. In the meantime, as a professional hunter for the Union Pacific Railroad, he took a major part in the slaughter of the American buffalo, which he regretted in later years.

Below: "Buffalo Bill" Cody, pictured in Paris in 1889. His Wild West Show was popular in Europe as well as America.

Bottom: Colorful poster advertising Buffalo Bill's Wild West Show, illustrating the use of authentic Indians in the show, some of them armed with Winchester rifles.

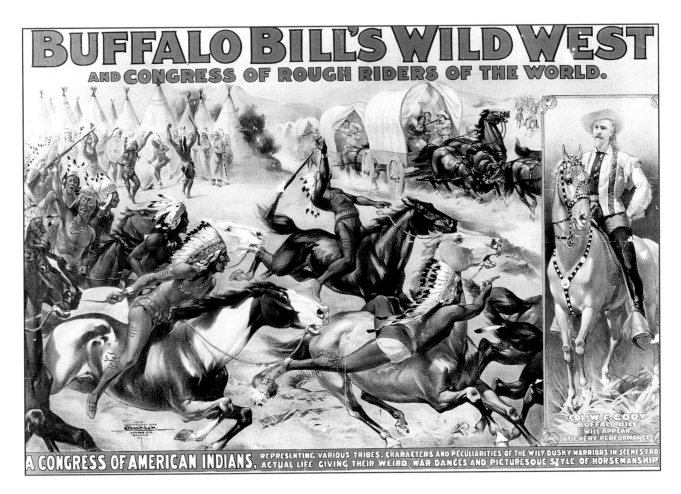

Of Annie Oakley, there is the colorful story concerning the incident in which she shot a cigarette out of the mouth of Crown Prince William, later Kaiser Wilhelm of Germany, stirring speculation as to what would have happened with World War I if she had missed and killed the Crown Prince!

Winchester rifles were used all over the world. Henry M. Stanley, in *How I Found Livingstone in Central Africa*, related how he left Zanzibar with a Henry rifle, which he left with Dr. Livingstone after finding him, and a Model 1866 Winchester. Professor Williamson in *Winchester, The Gun That Won The West*, cites a report by Major Ned H. Roberts from a trip to the Hudson Bay country of Canada in the late 1880s that the great majority of hunters and trappers were using the .44-40 Winchester Model 1873, "with which they killed all kinds of big game. The .44-40 cartridges were then practically the only ones you could be sure of finding in every Hudson Bay trading post in the country."

Extensive use of Winchester rifles was made by mining companies in different parts of the United States, as pointed out by Harold L. Bailey, Jr., in an article in the *Journal of the American Society of Arms Collectors*. He documents orders for Model 1873 rifles by companies in the coal mining regions of Pennsylvania, where the "Molly Maguires," an Irish group, led violent opposition to miners' working conditions. Homestake Mining, the leading gold producer, and the Anaconda Copper Company made extensive use of Winchesters for guard purposes and also, for better or worse, to combat the formation of labor unions.

The Model 1876

The Model 1873 rifle was prized for its large magazine capacity and rapid fire capability, but was not effective against big game or for military and defense use at ranges over 150 yards. The Army's .45-70 cartridge, with a powder charge of 70 grains and a bullet weighing 405 grains, could be fired accurately at a range of 600 yards or more. Remington, Sharps, and Whitney were all making civilian single-shot rifles in this caliber.

To meet this market, and in a further attempt to win Government contracts for military use, Winchester came out with a larger and stronger version of the Model 1873, called the Model 1876. Because of the limitations of the toggle-link mechanism, the cartridge it was designed to use, the .45-75 Winchester, did not have as large a bullet, at 350 grains, as the .45-70, but the powder charge was slightly larger, 75 grains. It was enthusiastically adopted by hunters, such as Theodore Roosevelt, and also by the Royal Canadian

Northwest Mounted Police, with whom it remained their official rifle until 1914.

The new rifle was exhibited at the Philadelphia Centennial Exposition held in the summer of 1876, and is sometimes known as the "Centennial Model." In 1878 the company's catalog described the Model 1876 as follows:

"The constant calls from many sources, and particularly from the regions in which the grizzly bear and other large game are found, as well as the plains where the absence of cover and shyness of some require the hunter to make his shots at long range, made it desirable for the Company to build a still more powerful gun than the Model 73."

The Model 1876 was not as popular as the Model 1873, which continued to be made during the period of production of the Model 1876. The toggle-link mechanism was a problem for use with higher power cartridges, and the solution came later with John Browning and the Model 1886.

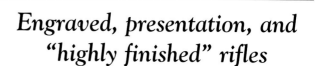

Engraved, presentation, and "highly finished" rifles

Winchester rifles with engraving on the receivers and other parts and with special features such as burl walnut stocks are often found, and are highly prized by collectors. Even today, Winchester maintains a Custom Gun Shop for special orders, and in recent years issued specially decorated and inscribed Commemorative models with considerable success.

The tradition of engraving goes back to the middle 1850s, when craftsmen especially from Germany were engaged by arms manufacturers, either directly or under contract.

Right: The Marquis De Mores, a neighbor of Theodore Roosevelt and fellow rancher in the Dakota territory, with his Model 1876 Winchester rifle. He and Roosevelt nearly fought a duel with Winchester rifles, but ended up as friends.

Below: Winchester Model 1876 rifle in .40-60 W.C.F. caliber, octagonal barrel with full magazine and single set trigger, equipped with sling swivels.

Bottom: Model 1876 octagonal barrel rifle, with leather scabbard for long-barreled rifle, and a .45-60 caliber round.

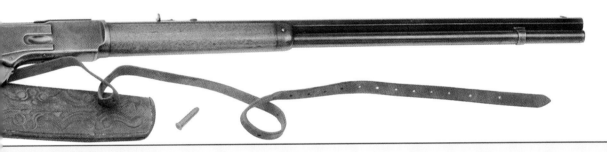

MODEL 1876

Type: 12-shot rifle; 9-shot carbine; 11-shot express rifle; 13-shot musket.

Made: 1876-1897.

Variations: First model, serial to about 3000, no dust cover. Early second model, serial to about 7000, dust cover guide rail screwed to top of frame; late second model, to serial about 30000, finger grip instead of thumbpiece on the dust cover. Third model, serial from about 30000 to end of production, guide rail is integral with the frame. A limited number of Northwest Mounted Police Carbines, with NWMP stamped on the buttstock, in .45-75 caliber; also 54 "One of 1000" and 8 "One of 100" models were made.

Quantity: 63,871.

Caliber: .40-60, .45-60, .45-75, and .50-95.

Barrel length: Sporting rifle 28 inches, carbine 22 inches, express rifle 26 inches, musket 32 inches. Barrels were supplied in standard, heavy, and extra heavy weights.

Markings: WINCHESTER'S REPEATING-ARMS, NEW HAVEN. CT. KING'S IMPROVEMENT PATENTED MARCH 19, 1866. OCTOBER 16, 1860.
Serial numbers on the lower tang. Barrel blued, receiver case hardened.

Mechanical function: Similar to the Model 1873, but the frames and other parts are noticeably larger, to accommodate the larger cartridges.

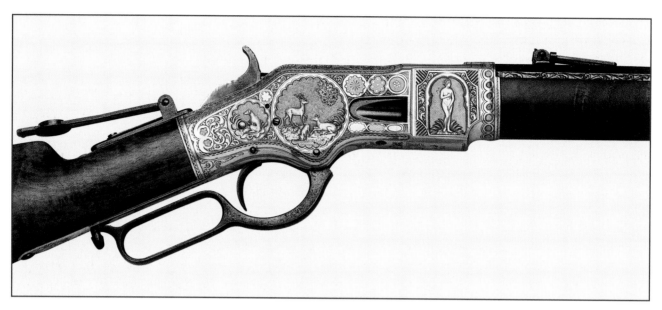

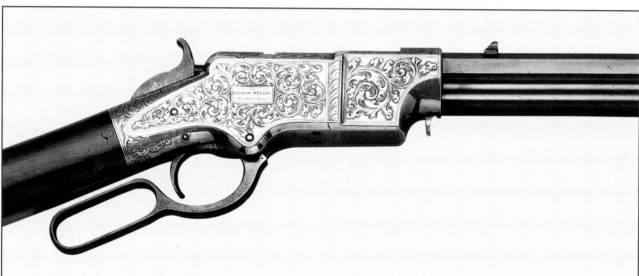

Above: Engraved Henry rifle, serial number 9, one of the earliest examples of Winchester engraving which carried through its later models. Presented to Gideon Welles, Secretary of the Navy, in the hope, largely vain, of obtaining military contracts.

Below: Gold plated and engraved Model 1866, probably made as a factory show gun and probably engraved by the master Gustave Young. The intricately crafted Statue of Liberty image was taken from banknote engraving of the time.

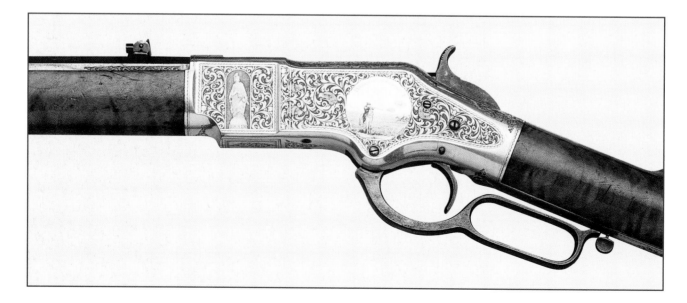

Left: Model 1866 rifle, serial number 79944, engraved by C. F. Ulrich, a protégé of Gustave Young. The female nude is in a similar pose to Hiram Powers' The Greek Slave.

Customers could obtain specially decorated arms for an extra charge, and also arms would be made up for presentation to potential customers. Samuel Colt was particularly known for this practice and Oliver Winchester followed suit, although at a lower key. At the beginning of the Civil War he presented his Serial No. 1 Henry rifle to Edwin M. Stanton, Union Secretary of War, and No. 6 to Abraham Lincoln. Serial No. 9 went to Gideon Welles, Secretary of the Navy.

In the late 1860s the charge made by Winchester for adding engraving was too high for most purchasers. Independent engravers were used by those desiring extra decoration; most notable among them was Louis D. Nimschke of New York City. A number of examples of his work with beautifully engraved panel scenes have survived,

as well as his pattern book. Nimschke also did relief work, cutting away the metal to produce a three-dimensional effect. He is particularly known for his work on Colt arms.

Starting in 1870, however, increased demand for engraved rifles led Winchester to employ what became a famous family of engravers, the Ulrichs. Herman Ulrich was hired in 1870, having completed his apprenticeship at Colt's, probably with Gustave Young. His older brother Conrad was soon brought in also, and then in 1875 a third brother, John, was engaged. The three brothers continued to work either full time or under contract until 1914. John appears to have been the least talented, and is credited for numerous engravings where his signature appears but which were actually done by others, according to Houze in his Winchester history. Other engravers were brought in as well, such as William E. Stokes. Noted engravers after World War I included Conrad's son Alden Ulrich and Rudolph J. Kornbrath. Herman Ulrich became a successful New York stockbroker from 1881 to 1889.

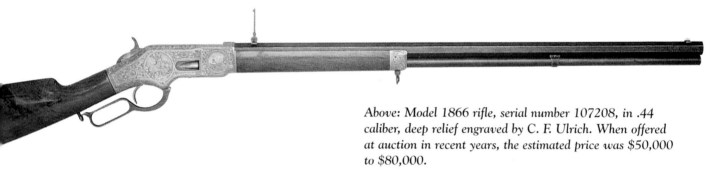

Above: Model 1866 rifle, serial number 107208, in .44 caliber, deep relief engraved by C. F. Ulrich. When offered at auction in recent years, the estimated price was $50,000 to $80,000.

Below: Closeup of panel scenes on the above model 1866 rifle, showing a doe and fawn, a hunting dog, and a bull elk. The name of the engraver C. F. Ulrich is stamped on the tang.

EXPANSION AND DIVERSIFICATION THROUGH THE TURN OF THE CENTURY

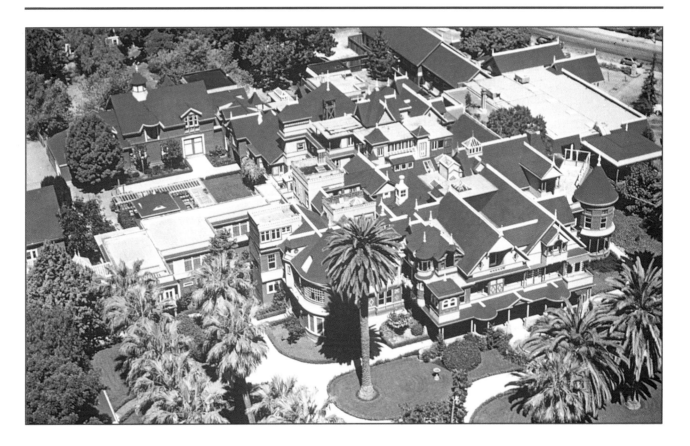

The death of Oliver Winchester in 1880 marked the end of a phenomenally successful career in arms manufacturing. From the small, struggling Volcanic Repeating Arms Company with no real assets except a patented idea, Winchester's company had now grown to nearly 700 employees and world leadership in the production of lever action repeating rifles. Another major accomplishment, not common in American industry, was keeping control of the company in the Winchester family, developing successors who maintained the company's progress right through the end of World War I.

Retirement evidently had no attraction for Oliver Winchester. He remained active as company president until age 69, and withdrew in 1879 only because of ill health. He had groomed his son, William Wirt Winchester, to succeed him, but William Wirt was already ill from tuberculosis and died only a few months later. However, two more family members were ready. William W. Converse, the husband of Mrs. William Wirt Winchester's sister, served as company

Above: Air view of the Winchester Mystery House, built over a period of more than twenty years by the eccentric widow of Oliver Winchester's son William Wirt. It may be visited as a major tourist attraction in San Jose, California.

president up to his death in 1889. After that, at age 55, T. G. Bennett, Oliver's son-in-law, who had been third in line during the latter part of Oliver's administration, served as company president until 1918*, finally retiring at age 73 with the sale of the company. A majority of the company stock was held by family members until that time.

Professor Williamson in *Winchester, The Gun That Won The West*, comments that little could be found about Oliver Winchester's personal life. He was not known, for example, as a marksman or hunter, as might have been expected, but seems to have been completely devoted to business. He did make substantial contributions to Yale University, as did his family; he gave the present Observatory building in 1879,

* From 1910 to 1918 the nominal presidents were George E. Hodson and Winchester Bennett, the son of T.G., but T.G. stayed actively involved, and again became president briefly in 1918, before the company was sold.

and his wife later gave Winchester Hall and also a substantial donation to the Yale Art School. Another family member gave a large donation to the Yale Medical School.

Outside of Yale University, the most visible legacy of the Winchester family is the Winchester Mystery House in San Jose, California, now a major tourist attraction in the Santa Clara ("Silicon") Valley. This is a 160-room mansion on what was originally a 162 acre fruit farm. It was built by Sarah Winchester, William Wirt's widow. The story is that after the death of her only child, a daughter, shortly after her husband's death, she was despondent and consulted a spiritualist or medium. The medium apparently convinced her that the spirits of all those who had been killed by the rifles her family had manufactured had sought their revenge by killing her loved ones, and would haunt her unless she could escape. Having inherited $20,000,000 and 48 percent of the Winchester company stock, she was able to move to California and to continuously build a house, which she apparently thought would stop the spirits.

The house is a marvel of Victorian architecture, although bizarre. It grew with no plan, apparently directed only by what the spirits told Mrs. Winchester. There are rooms with no interconnections, doors and windows opening onto blank walls, and stairways going into the ceiling. The number 13 recurs, such as in the windows in a particular room, candles on a chandelier, or steps in a staircase. The house was damaged in the earthquake which destroyed much of San Francisco in 1906, but Mrs. Winchester kept on building until her death in 1928.

Living alone with only a niece and her staff, Sarah Winchester was considered eccentric if not worse, but at the same time she carried on extensive works of charity such as establishing a tuberculosis hospital. Today the property is the Winchester Mystery House Gardens and Historical Museum, with an active management providing continuous tours and maintaining a collection of Winchester firearms. A visit is highly recommended; for example, the house is reputed to have one of the finest and largest collections of art glass doors and windows in the world.

Referring back to the Winchester company, its continuing success after 1880 can be appreciated by considering its competition. Three of Winchester's competitors were also located in Connecticut: Colt's Patent Firearms Manufacturing Company in Hartford, and the Whitney Arms Company and Marlin Firearms in New Haven. Smith & Wesson was located in Springfield, Massachusetts, and E. Remington & Sons in Ilion, New York. Only Smith & Wesson had no interest in producing

Below: 1886 Winchester factory cartridge board made for advertising purposes, with a total of 119 cartridges, both rimfire and centerfire, for rifles and pistols. The design is known to collectors as the "Inverted V Board." Shotshells are also included.

rifles; the company was competing with Colt's in handguns, having received orders from Russia for over 100,000 of its .44 caliber single action revolvers.

The Whitney company was founded in 1798 by Eli Whitney, who had invented (but not profited from) the cotton gin in 1793. He was succeeded in 1825 by his son Eli Whitney, Jr., who continued to develop the company through the Civil War, where it was a major arms contractor. After the Civil War Whitney developed a series of single-shot and also lever action rifles, some of which were sold overseas for military use. However, with advancing age and declining company sales, he sold the company to Winchester in 1888.

Marlin Firearms was founded by a former Colt's employee, John M. Marlin, in 1863. He first made small handguns, but in 1873 bought the Brown Manufacturing Company of Newburyport,

Above: William Mason, who assisted Colt's with the development of the 1873 Peacemaker revolver and then, as a Winchester employee, developed finished arms from John Browning's crude designs.

Massachusetts, which made the popular Ballard target and sporting rifles. By 1890, Marlin began to concentrate on lever action rifles and pump action shotguns, and the company's products still compete with Winchester lever action rifles. However, Marlin production up to World War I was small compared with Winchester's.

Like Whitney, Remington has historic early roots, dating from 1816, when Eliphalet Remington II began to make gun barrels. The company was a major producer of muskets and revolvers in the Civil War, and from 1867 to 1888 produced a huge number of rolling block single-shot rifles, with over a million being sold in the United States and overseas. As the single-shot rifle became obsolete for military use the company was in financial straits, and in 1888 was purchased jointly by Winchester and by Schuyler, Hartley and Graham of New York, which also owned the large Union Metallic Cartridge Company. The partnership continued until 1896, when Winchester withdrew and Marcellus Hartley continued as president. The company became a major contractor in World War I, merged with UMC Cartridge, was owned by the Dupont Corporation from 1933 to 1993, and is now a major Winchester competitor.

In 1880, Colt's was substantially larger than Winchester – it had up to 1,400 employees as early as the Civil War, while Winchester had some 700 employees in 1880. But Colt's primarily made revolvers as against Winchester's rifles until 1883, when Colt's came out with the Colt-Burgess Lever Action Rifle. There is a colorful story as to how this came about, and how after only two years and a production of only about 6,000 rifles, Colt suddenly stopped production of this rifle and left the lever action field to Winchester.

The Colt company's purchase of Andrew Burgess's patents and the start of production of the Colt-Burgess lever action rifle in 1883 was in retaliation for a competitive tactic Winchester had used against the double barrel shotgun introduced by Colt's in 1878. Beginning in 1880, Winchester began selling a large quantity of imported English shotguns at its New York City Sales Agency, undercutting the price of shotguns produced by Colt's. Also, hearing about the Colt company's purchase of the Burgess patent, Winchester started its own retaliation by importing 600 Webley double action revolvers from England, again undercutting a Colt's arm, the double action Frontier

Above: Single action revolver designed by Mason for Winchester in 1883 as a potential competitor for Colt's. The threat of this potential competition led Colt's to withdraw from the lever action rifle market.

Right: Corresponding double action revolver also developed by Winchester, attributed to former Smith & Wesson inventor William Wetmore. Winchester agreed with Colt's that it would not go into the revolver market.

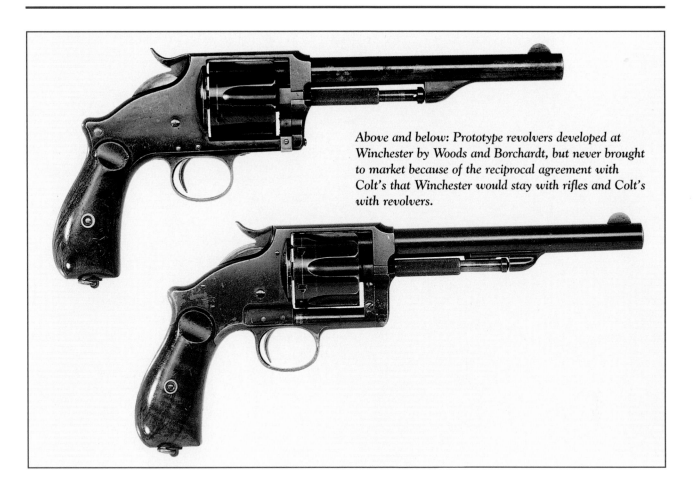

Above and below: Prototype revolvers developed at Winchester by Woods and Borchardt, but never brought to market because of the reciprocal agreement with Colt's that Winchester would stay with rifles and Colt's with revolvers.

revolver. In addition, having hired a top designer from Colt's, William Mason, in 1882, Winchester had Mason design a new single action revolver designed to compete with Colt's Peacemaker, and a slide action rifle designed to compete with the Lightning slide action rifle which Colt had under development.

The matter was resolved, T .G. Bennett of Winchester later told Edwin Pugsley, the Winchester general superintendent, by a personal meeting between the Winchester and Colt's chief executives. Bennett innocently asked the Colt's executives what they thought of Mason's pistol models, which he had conveniently brought with him.

After a lengthy discussion of pistols and rifles, the joint conclusion was reached that Colt could not make any money from lever action rifles and Winchester could not make any money from pistols, so a "gentleman's agreement" was made that each would stay out of the other's business in this regard. The agreement has always been maintained: Winchester never produced pistols after that,*

and Colt's never produced a lever action rifle after the Burgess. Winchester did produce a successful slide action rifle starting in 1890, but only in .22 caliber, and the Colt Lightning slide action rifle was produced only up to 1898, with limited success.

William Mason and Edwin Pugsley were both outstanding employees of Winchester. Born in 1837, Mason worked for both the Colt and Remington companies as a designer and was an independent contractor during the Civil War, making Springfield type rifle muskets. For Colt's in particular, he was issued several patents for the successful development of the 1873 Peacemaker revolver. He produced important innovations and improvements at Winchester in machinery as well as arms, and when Winchester later bought a series of John Browning's spectacular inventions, it was Mason who made these into workable designs from Browning's crude models. He ranks close to Browning as an arms inventor.

Edwin Pugsley had a lifelong career at Winchester, which he joined out of Yale and Massachusetts Institute of Technology in 1911. He was the general superintendent up until the 1950s, and was known as a conscientious administrator and capable designer. He also had a large personal arms collection, which he sold to the Winchester Company Museum in 1950, and which is now at the Buffalo

---

* Before Mason was brought in, Winchester designers Wetmore and Wood invented a revolver, of which 30,000 were ordered by Turkey in 1877.

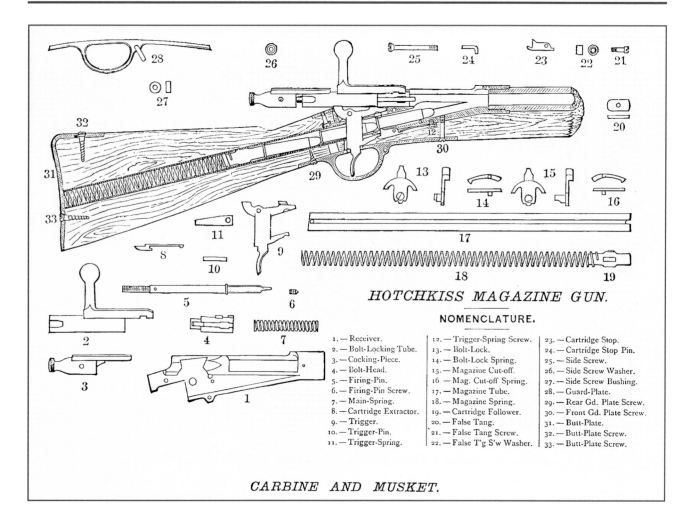

HOTCHKISS MAGAZINE GUN.

NOMENCLATURE.

1. — Receiver.	12. — Trigger-Spring Screw.	23. — Cartridge Stop.
2. — Bolt-Locking Tube.	13. — Bolt-Lock.	24. — Cartridge Stop Pin.
3. — Cocking-Piece.	14. — Bolt-Lock Spring.	25. — Side Screw.
4. — Bolt-Head.	15. — Magazine Cut-off.	26. — Side Screw Washer.
5. — Firing-Pin.	16. — Mag. Cut-off Spring.	27. — Side Screw Bushing.
6. — Firing-Pin Screw.	17. — Magazine Tube.	28. — Guard-Plate.
7. — Main-Spring.	18. — Magazine Spring.	29. — Rear Gd. Plate Screw.
8. — Cartridge Extractor.	19. — Cartridge Follower.	30. — Front Gd. Plate Screw.
9. — Trigger.	20. — False Tang.	31. — Butt-Plate.
10. — Trigger-Pin.	21. — False Tang Screw.	32. — Butt-Plate Screw.
11. — Trigger-Spring.	22. — False T'g S'w Washer.	33. — Butt-Plate Screw.

CARBINE AND MUSKET.

Bill Historical Center in Cody, Wyoming. As an incidental note, he was a stocky man with a bulldog appearance and also a sense of humor. His close friend and fellow arms collector Charles Addams named his Addams Family character "Pugsley" after him.

The rest of Winchester's history up to World War I is best told in terms of the greatly expanded line of rifles and shotguns it produced. The competitive position of the company, together with its capable management, allowed it to take full advantage of the expansion of American shooting sports during this period. Hunting game with rifles and birds with shotguns were popular sports, in addition to which there was a proliferation of clubs and competitions in target shooting, much of this related to the German tradition of "Schuetzen" shooting and social clubs.

The Hotchkiss rifle

Oliver Winchester always kept an eye out for potential military contracts, and although the Army adopted the .45-70 cartridge and the single-shot trapdoor Springfield rifle in 1873, there was clearly a need for a repeating rifle which could use this powerful cartridge. In 1877 he bought the rights to a bolt action rifle designed by Benjamin B. Hotchkiss, whom Winchester had met at the Philadelphia

Centennial Exhibition. This is the same Hotchkiss who later invented a crank-operated heavy machine gun adopted by the U.S. Navy.

Improvements to the Hotchkiss were made by the Winchester designers between Army trials from 1878 to 1883, when the Army ordered 750 Hotchkiss rifles and the Navy 2,500. The two services also ordered bolt action rifles made by James Paris Lee and the Remington Arms Company, and Chaffee-Reese bolt action rifles made by the Springfield Armory . Of the three systems for the .45-70 cartridge, Remington's was the most successful in that over 100,000 were produced, mainly for export. The Winchester Hotchkiss was only moderately successful for civilian sale.

John M. Browning and the Winchester single-shot rifle

The spectacularly fruitful association between Winchester and legendary arms designer John M. Browning began with the company's recognition of the need to add a single-shot rifle to its sales line. The Sharps falling block system effectively used for carbines in the Civil War had proved adaptable to the high power centerfire .45-70 cartridge, and in the period around 1880 the Sharps was the principal rifle

Left: How the Hotchkiss rifle worked, from the September 1882 Winchester catalog; magazine in buttstock, with the cartridges loaded into the chamber and ejected by a bolt action mechanism. The rifle used the powerful military 45-70 cartridge

Right: Early Winchester gunsights, showing the variety of civilian and military arms offered by Winchester, from target shooting through hunting to use by the Army. The sport of target shooting was particularly popular at the time.

used in slaughtering the American buffalo to the point of extinction. However, its side-mounted hammer was cumbersome and had become obsolete. Also, the great interest in target shooting – R. L. Wilson likens this to golf today, with the Creedmoor Range on Long Island outside New York City, like the site of the Master's – created a need for a new rifle which could be adapted to the super accurate "Schuetzen" style.

A simple, practical, new single-shot rifle was invented by the 23-year-old John M. Browning in Ogden, Utah, in 1878, and was patented the following year. For Browning, this was the first in a series of brilliant inventions he was to make all they way up to his death in 1926, for Winchester, Colt's, Fabrique

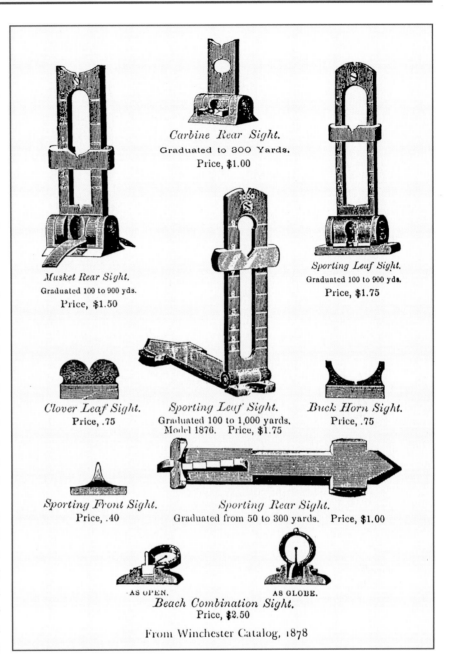

Carbine Rear Sight.
Graduated to 300 Yards.
Price, $1.00

Musket Rear Sight.
Graduated 100 to 900 yds.
Price, $1.50

Sporting Leaf Sight.
Graduated 100 to 900 yds.
Price, $1.75

Clover Leaf Sight.
Price, .75

Sporting Leaf Sight.
Graduated 100 to 1,000 yards.
Model 1876.   Price, $1.75

Buck Horn Sight.
Price, .75

Sporting Front Sight.
Price, .40

Sporting Rear Sight.
Graduated from 50 to 300 yards.   Price, $1.00

AS OPEN.   AS GLOBE.
Beach Combination Sight.
Price, $2.50

From Winchester Catalog, 1878

HOTCHKISS RIFLE

Type: Seven-shot bolt action rifle, musket, and carbine.
Made: 1879-1899.
Variations: First model, serial to about 6419, one-piece stock with circular cutoff device on right side above the trigger guard. Second model, serial to 22521, safety at top of left side of receiver, magazine cutoff on the top right side behind bolt handle. Third model, serial to 84555, two-piece stock with exposed receiver. A small number of first and second models with military markings apparently made at the Springfield Armory.

Quantity: 84,555, most for military use, U.S. and foreign.

Caliber: .45-70.

Barrel length: Sporting rifle 26 inches, musket 32 inches, carbine 24 inches.

Markings: On side of receiver, MANUFACTURED BY THE WINCHESTER REPEATING ARMS CO. NEW HAVEN CONN. U.S.A. PATENTED OCT 16, 1863, JUNE 18, 1863. JUNE 25, 1872. JULY 23, 1878, AND UNDER B. HOTCHKISS' PAT'S AUG.17, 1869, FEB. 15, 1870, NOV. 9, 1875, NOV. 14, 1876, JAN.23, 1877. Serial number at rear of receiver.

Mechanical function: Six shots in the butt, loaded individually from the top of the receiver. Magazine cutoff allows operation as single-shot. Bolt handle extends out to the side, and is worked by turning to vertical position and pulling back to cock and to eject a used cartridge if present, then pushing forward and turning to load a fresh cartridge and lock the action.

Above: John Browning's workbench in the Browning Gun Factory in Ogden, Utah, where he developed 44 patents for revolutionary new firearms over a period of over 20 years, all bought by Winchester.

Nationale (FN) in Belgium, and his own Browning Arms Company. His inventive genius has been compared to Edison and Marconi, and his firearms ranged from his first single-shot rifle to machine cannons. All of Winchester's new designs starting in 1885 were based on Browning's inventions, up to the time of his breakup with Winchester in 1902 over his automatic shotgun, as related below.

John Moses Browning was a Mormon by background, his father having had three wives and a total of 17 children. John and three of his brothers followed in their father's footsteps as gunsmiths. In the book *John M. Browning, American Gunmaker*, his son relates how John had an aptitude for understanding smallarms mechanisms as early as age 10, when he wired together an old gun barrel and some discarded parts and shot three prairie chickens for dinner. John seldom used blueprints for his designs even in later years, being able to visualize how gun parts related to each other and to fabricate them directly at his workbench.

After John had patented his new single-shot rifle, he and his three brothers, who had inherited their father's gun shop, decided to set up their own manufacturing operation, even though John was frustrated in not being able to spend more time on inventing more arms. Several hundred of the Browning single-shot rifles were produced at the brothers' shop, where they  also made ends meet by selling ammunition and fishing tackle. In 1883, however, the Winchester company bought the rifle's patent from Browning for the then substantial sum of $8,000. The purchase also included a Winchester dealership for the Brownings and John's agreement to give Winchester the right of first refusal on his subsequent rifle inventions. The story by John's son is that a Winchester salesman bought one of the Browning guns for fifteen dollars and sent it to T. G. Bennett, the Winchester president, who was so impressed that he went by train to see John personally and arrange their deal.

Browning's single shot-rifle was popular and continued in production by Winchester until 1920.

continued on page 60

Right: John Browning in later life. He was modest, unassuming, and hardworking, dying of a heart attack at his workbench in the FN plant in Herstal, Belgium.

Below: Winchester single-shot musket (2nd Model High Wall) built on an action by John Browning and introduced 1885: lever-operated, dropping-block, first of many Browning designs to be made by Winchester. Over 28 years' production, 109,327 of these elegant rifles were built in a variety of configurations and 59 calibers. Shown above rifle is an original box of Winchester "Lesmoke" .22 cartridges.

MODEL 1885 SINGLE-SHOT RIFLE

Type: Lever action falling block rifle, also made as a shotgun. Made: 1885-1920.

Variations: Many variations in size and details, but the basic division is between High Wall, with the receiver largely covering the hammer, and Low Wall, with more of the hammer assembly exposed. Further variation between "thickside" frames with flat sides not flaring out to meet the stock, and "thinside," with the sides thinner and flared out to meet the stock. Shotgun made in High Wall only. Musket in .22 caliber known as the Winder, after an Army officer who assisted in its design, and purchased by the Army for training.

Some rifles made in "Schuetzen" style with features such as spurs on the buttplate, elaborate finger levers, and special triggers.

Quantity: Approximately 139,725.

Caliber: A wide range, from .22 to .50 centerfire.

Barrel length: Rifles 24 inches to 30 inches, musket 28 inches, "Schuetzen" 30 inches.

Markings: Winchester and patent and trademark data; caliber designation at breech end of barrel. Serial number on lower

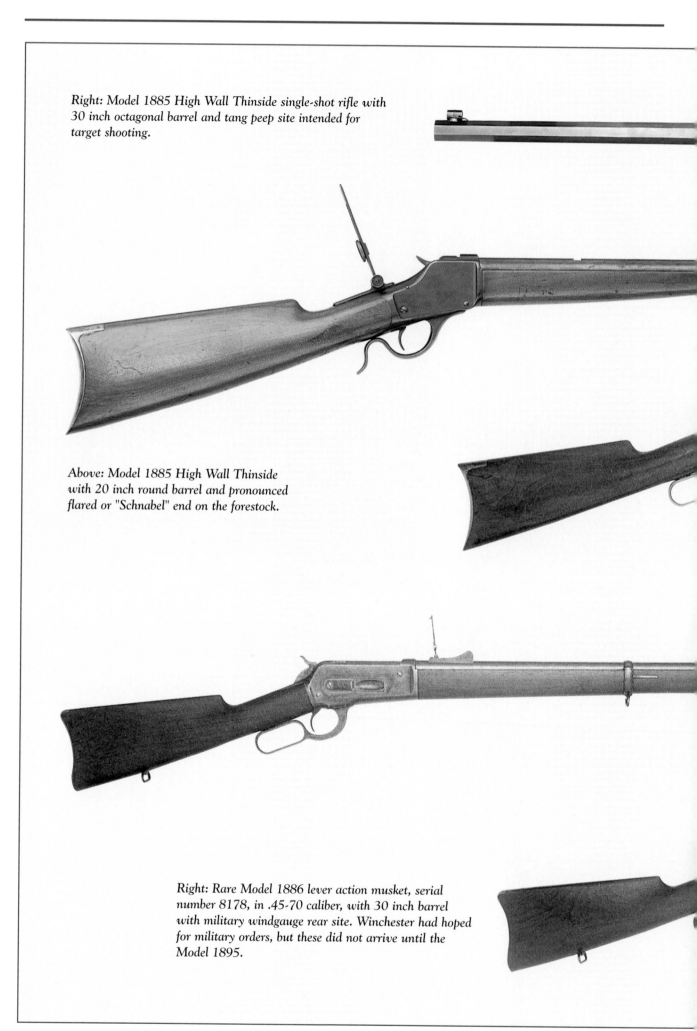

Right: Model 1885 High Wall Thinside single-shot rifle with 30 inch octagonal barrel and tang peep site intended for target shooting.

Above: Model 1885 High Wall Thinside with 20 inch round barrel and pronounced flared or "Schnabel" end on the forestock.

Right: Rare Model 1886 lever action musket, serial number 8178, in .45-70 caliber, with 30 inch barrel with military windgauge rear site. Winchester had hoped for military orders, but these did not arrive until the Model 1895.

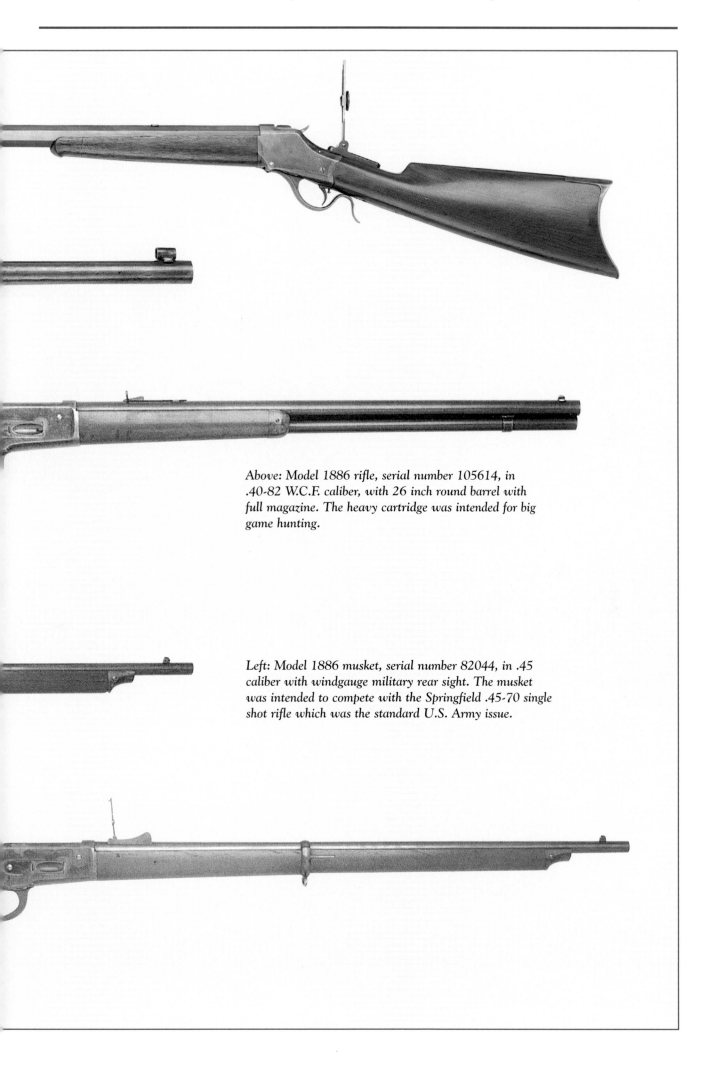

Above: Model 1886 rifle, serial number 105614, in .40-82 W.C.F. caliber, with 26 inch round barrel with full magazine. The heavy cartridge was intended for big game hunting.

Left: Model 1886 musket, serial number 82044, in .45 caliber with windgauge military rear sight. The musket was intended to compete with the Springfield .45-70 single shot rifle which was the standard U.S. Army issue.

The Model 1886 rifle

After selling his single-shot rifle patent to the Winchester company in 1883, John Browning could proceed with the more significant invention he had been impatient to develop while he and his brothers were carrying on their manufacturing operation (the unsophisticated brothers were startled to learn from Winchester that they had to stop making their own single-shot rifles, since Winchester now had the patent). The new invention was what would become the Model 1886 lever action rifle, badly needed by Winchester since their previous models could not satisfactorily handle high power cartridges. John obtained his patent in October 1884, and immediately left, with his brother Matt, for their first trip East to take the new gun to Winchester. T. G. Bennett agreed to pay them the amount of $50,000, which John later described as "more money than there is in all of Ogden."

The following chapter describes the success of the Model 1886 and other Winchesters as hunting guns used by Theodore Roosevelt and other notables. The Model 1886 dominated the market for this type of arm and also led to the still more popular Models 1892 and 1894, which eventually replaced the venerable Model 1873.

It is noteworthy that during the entire period of Winchester's association with Browning, nearly 20 years, Winchester bought all of Browning's rifle patents, 44 in number, although actually using only 10. This was partly because some of the designs would not have been practical, but mostly in order to prevent these inventions from getting into the hands of competitors. Credit should be given at the same time, however, to Winchester's own engineers such as William Mason. Browning delivered only crude models showing the basic principles involved, after which the actual designs for production had to be developed.

Above: Chief Fine Wolf with a new case-hardened Model 1886 rifle, posed also with a cartridge belt and a Colt single-action revolver, and also a peace pipe indicating that his intentions are not necessarily hostile!

THE MODEL 1886 RIFLE

Type: Lever action rifle, carbine, and musket, tubular magazine, number of shots varying with model.

Made: 1886 to 1935.

Variations: Basic model unchanged, but some made as "Extra Light Weight" with tapered barrel, half magazine, and rubber shotgun buttplate, and some rifles as a takedown model coming apart at the forward end of the breech.

Quantity: approximately 47,000 to 54,000.
Caliber: range from .33 W.C.F. to .50.
Barrel length: rifle 26 inches, carbine 22 inches, musket 30 inches.

Markings: Winchester name and address and patent and trademark data; Model 1886 usually on upper tang; serial numbers on lower tang. Blued finish except case hardened fittings on early production.

Mechanical function: The major change from earlier models was replacing the horizontal toggle-link system of connecting the lever, hammer, and carrier with a vertical action with twin locking bars riding in mortises cut in the sides of the receiver walls and the bolt. This provided positive locking to accommodate high power cartridges. The receiver was shortened and streamlined.

Models 1892 and 1894

Again based on Browning designs, these two lever action rifles modernized the Model 1873 to such an extent that the second, the Model 1894, is still in production today. The Model 1892 uses the Browning vertical action instead of the toggle-link system, and is stronger and lighter than the 1873. The Model 1894, with a squarer frame, uses a flat plate under the frame forward of the trigger assembly, that folds downward and moves a vertical link up and down to work the action. The characteristics of the rifle are similar to those of the Model 1886,

but it was designed for lighter caliber cartridges.

The Model 1892 was made from 1892 to 1941, with production approximately 1,000,000; and the Model 1894 was made from that year to the present, with production over 3,000,000. Calibers were .25-20 up to .44-40, with the largest number of the 1894 in .30-30, still the most popular deer hunting rifle in the United States. The rifles reached such a stage of perfection that there have been no model changes. For each, there have been takedown (barrel separating for easier carrying) and short Trapper's Model variations.

The Model 1894 was the first Winchester rifle specifically designed for the new smokeless gunpowder, although models

Above: Model 1892 carbine with "large loop" configuration. This is the actual carbine, serial number 987672, used by John Wayne in John Ford's 1939 film classic, "Stagecoach," and several later Westerns.

Right: Disassembly instructions for the Model 1886 rifle, from Winchester's 50th Anniversary Catalog of 1916. This illustrates the strong single vertical link which the lever operates, as contrasted to the toggle link mechanism of the earlier Winchester rifles.

Right: Instructions for the assembly of the Model 1866 rifle, illustrating the vertical link mechanism still more clearly. The cartridges can be seen in the magazine and on the carrier, ready to be inserted in the chamber. Instructions for the assembly of the Model 1866 rifle, illustrating the vertical link mechanism still more clearly. The cartridges can be seen in the magazine and on the carrier, ready to be inserted in the chamber.

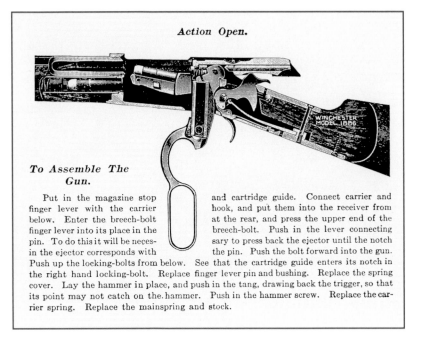

MODEL 1886

24

Winchester Repeating Rifle System.

Action Closed.

To Dismount The Gun.

Remove the stock. Unscrew strain screw. Drive out the mainspring from left to right. Remove the carrier spring. Take out the hammer screw and tang with sear attached. Draw out the hammer. Remove the spring cover. Drive out the finger lever pin and bushing. Draw the locking-bolts out from below. Pull back the breech-bolt until the lever connecting pin shows at the rear of the receiver. Drive out the pin. Draw out finger lever and carrier attached by the carrier hook. Remove the cartridge guide and magazine stop.

Action Open.

To Assemble The Gun.

Put in the magazine stop finger lever with the carrier below. Enter the breech-bolt finger lever into its place in the pin. To do this it will be necessary in the ejector corresponds with

and cartridge guide. Connect carrier and hook, and put them into the receiver from at the rear, and press the upper end of the breech-bolt. Push in the lever connecting sary to press back the ejector until the notch the pin. Push the bolt forward into the gun.

Push up the locking-bolts from below. See that the cartridge guide enters its notch in the right hand locking-bolt. Replace finger lever pin and bushing. Replace the spring cover. Lay the hammer in place, and push in the tang, drawing back the trigger, so that its point may not catch on the hammer. Push in the hammer screw. Replace the carrier spring. Replace the mainspring and stock.

BARRY

Above: Annie Oakley, "Little Sure Shot," with a deluxe, engraved Model 1892 rifle with a half round, half octagonal barrel. Featured in Buffalo Bill's Wild West Show, she was also the subject of a popular 20th century musical, "Annie get Your Gun."

Right: A young hunter and his attractive companion, in the West of the late 1800s. His rifle is a Winchester carbine, probably Model 1892 or 94. Boys were introduced to hunting at an early age, and still are even today in the West.

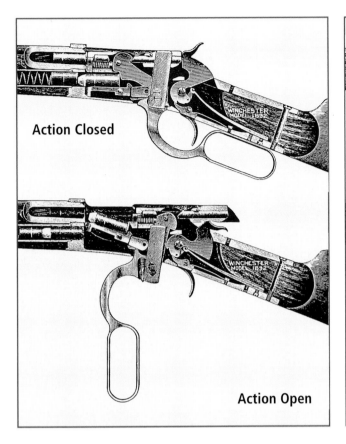

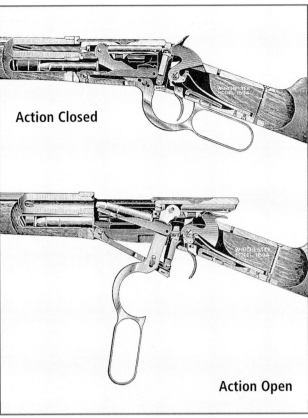

Above: Diagrams of the action of the Model 1892 rifle, from the Winchester 1916 catalog. This is similar to the Model 1886 but more compact, adapted to taking lower powered cartridges for smaller game such as deer.

Above: The action of the Model 1894, which is still in production as a popular modern hunting rifle, using smokeless powder. The flat plat pivoting at the bottom of the breech distinguishes it from earlier models.

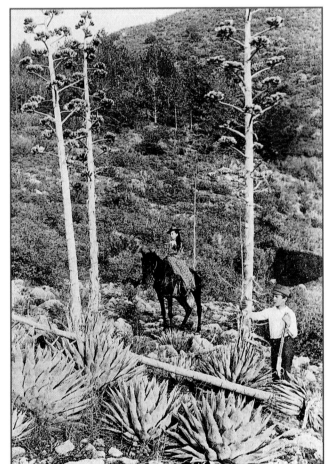

from the 1873 on were so well designed that scaled down smokeless powder cartridges could be used in them. The new powder was a major advance. The traditional black powder, made of charcoal, sulfur and saltpeter, emitted smoke which would alert an enemy or game, was subject to incomplete burning which left fouling in the bore, and had too fast a rate of combustion such that the bullet would lose velocity as it traveled through the barrel. Smokeless powder produces higher velocity, flatter trajectory, and better accuracy and range, besides leaving the gun bore cleaner. It was developed starting in 1885 by Alfred Nobel and others, by combining nitroglycerin and guncotton (nitrated cellulose). At the same time, bullet jacketing was introduced, to keep lead bullets from disintegrating.

Model 1895 rifle and the Winchester-Lee Straight Pull

The Model 1895 was the final Browning design of a large caliber lever action rifle, and was developed to take advantage of the new high power military and hunting cartridges with smokeless powder. A box magazine in front of

continued on page 66

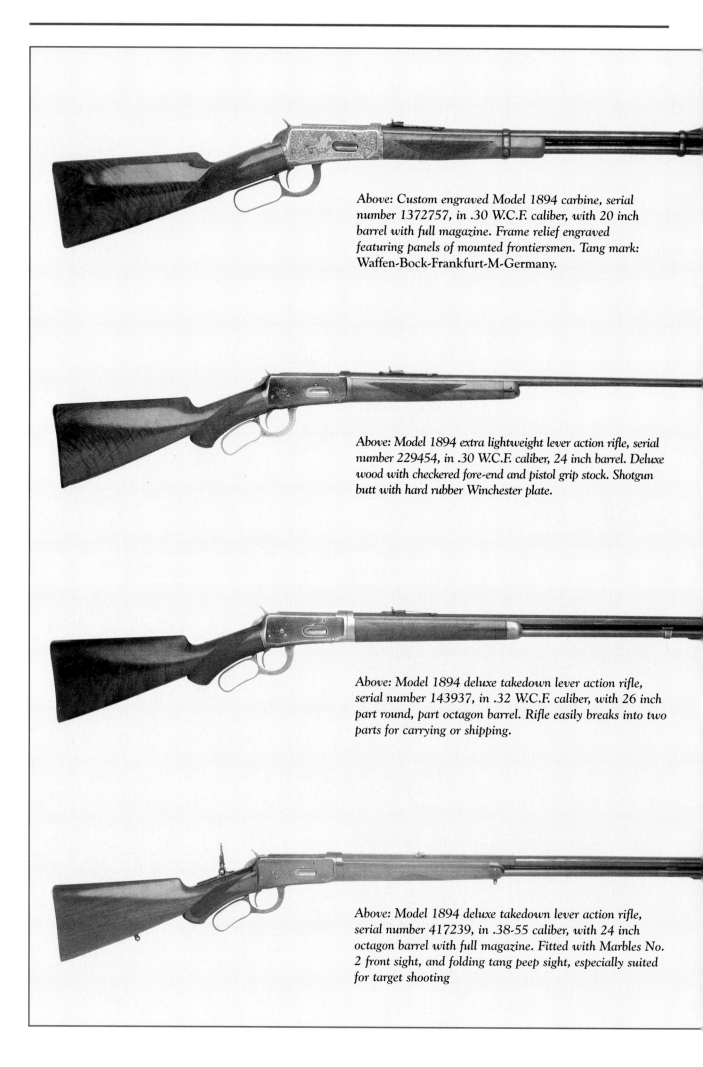

Above: Custom engraved Model 1894 carbine, serial number 1372757, in .30 W.C.F. caliber, with 20 inch barrel with full magazine. Frame relief engraved featuring panels of mounted frontiersmen. Tang mark: Waffen-Bock-Frankfurt-M-Germany.

Above: Model 1894 extra lightweight lever action rifle, serial number 229454, in .30 W.C.F. caliber, 24 inch barrel. Deluxe wood with checkered fore-end and pistol grip stock. Shotgun butt with hard rubber Winchester plate.

Above: Model 1894 deluxe takedown lever action rifle, serial number 143937, in .32 W.C.F. caliber, with 26 inch part round, part octagon barrel. Rifle easily breaks into two parts for carrying or shipping.

Above: Model 1894 deluxe takedown lever action rifle, serial number 417239, in .38-55 caliber, with 24 inch octagon barrel with full magazine. Fitted with Marbles No. 2 front sight, and folding tang peep sight, especially suited for target shooting

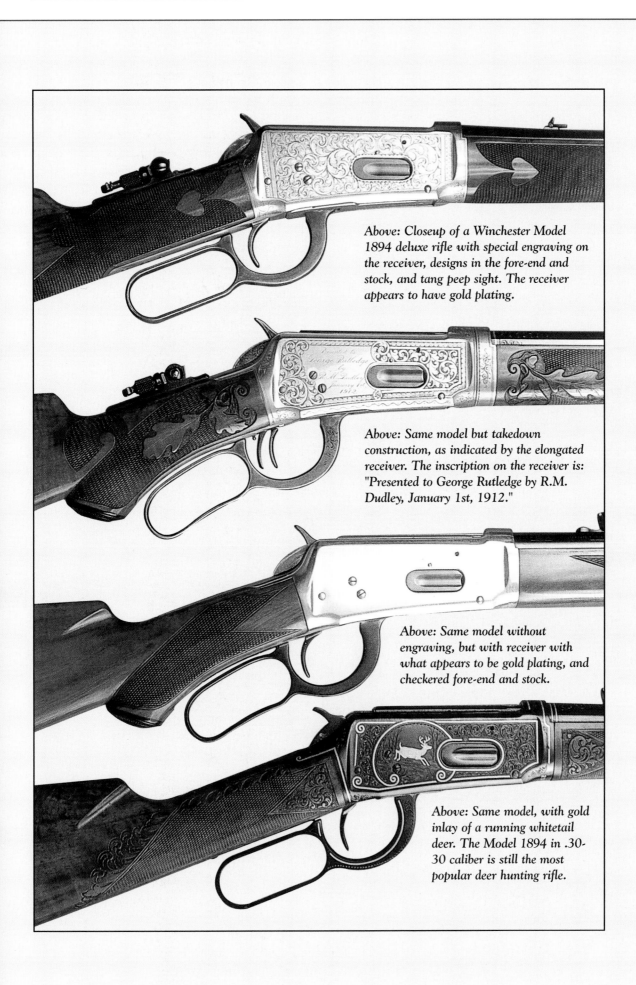

Above: Closeup of a Winchester Model 1894 deluxe rifle with special engraving on the receiver, designs in the fore-end and stock, and tang peep sight. The receiver appears to have gold plating.

Above: Same model but takedown construction, as indicated by the elongated receiver. The inscription on the receiver is: "Presented to George Rutledge by R.M. Dudley, January 1st, 1912."

Above: Same model without engraving, but with receiver with what appears to be gold plating, and checkered fore-end and stock.

Above: Same model, with gold inlay of a running whitetail deer. The Model 1894 in .30-30 caliber is still the most popular deer hunting rifle.

the trigger assembly was adopted because the new cartridges used pointed bullets which would be dangerous when stacked in a tubular magazine. Winchester was evidently hoping that it would compete with the bolt action Mauser type rifles which were being adopted around the world and the Krag rifle adopted by the U.S. Army in 1894. The Winchester Model 1895 rifle was successful in attracting a major overseas order from the Russians and was popular with hunters. Ironically, it was used by the Bolsheviks after World War I when a British and American expeditionary force tried unsuccessfully to stop the Communist revolution in Russia.

Winchester made another attempt to obtain military orders with the Lee Straight Pull Rifle, made from 1895 to 1902 with a production of about 20,000. The U.S. Navy, always more progressive than the Army, purchased 15,000 of this total, and the rifle saw much action with the Navy and the Marines in the Spanish-American War.

Winchester had acquired the patent from James Paris Lee, the inventor. The rifle was ahead of its time in using a small .236 caliber cartridge, and had an innovative bolt action in which only a short upward movement was needed before pulling the bolt back.

Below: Model 1895 box magazine rifle in sporting configuration, with tang rear sight, .45 caliber. This model in military configuration was sold to the Russian Government for use in World War I.

Shotguns and the end of the Browning connection

As described above in relation to the "gentleman's agreement" between Winchester and Colt's in which Winchester would not produce handguns and Colt's would not produce rifles, Winchester imported shotguns from England, in a quantity of about 10,000, from 1879 to 1894. These were marked "WINCHESTER REPEATING ARMS CO. NEW HAVEN, CONNECTICUT U.S.A.", along with the grade, which was marked A, B, C or D.

Winchester made no other attempt to go into the shotgun market until 1887, when a lever action shotgun that John Browning reluctantly agreed to design was released. The Model 1887 Shotgun was rather awkward in appearance, with a massive receiver and a five-shot magazine under the barrel, and had limited popularity. Total production from 1887 to 1901 was approximately 64,855. It was made in 10 and 12 gauge with 30 inch and 32 inch barrels, and also in riot gun form with a 20 inch barrel. It continued in production up to 1920, modified for smokeless powder loads, as the Model 1901, but in a quantity of only 13,500.

Where Winchester did achieve success in shotguns was with the slide action, again designed by Browning. The Model 1893, with a production of approximately 34,050, was

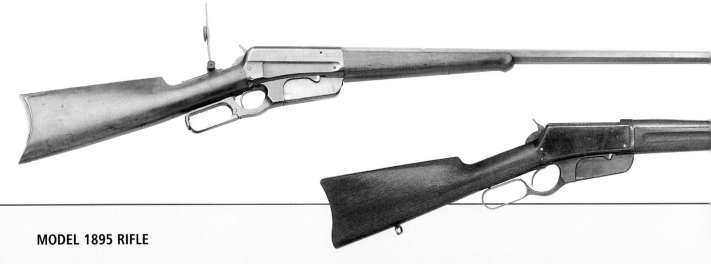

MODEL 1895 RIFLE

Type: Five- to six-shot lever action rifle, carbine, and musket, with box magazine.

Made 1896 to 1931.

Variations: Rifle to serial number about 5,000, "flatside," frame sides without scalloping or fluting; U.S. Army model in .30-40 caliber, full stock with hand guard, too late for the Spanish-American War, a few used in the Philippines; NRA Musket approved by the National Rifle Association for competitive use; Russian Model in 7.62mm caliber for the Russian Government.

Quantity: 425,881, including 293,816 made on order from the Russian Government and used in World War I.

Calibers: .30-40 and .30-06 U.S. Military, 7.62mm Russian, and .303 British, plus hunting calibers to .405 Winchester.

Barrel length: 22 inches to 28 inches.

Markings: Similar to those for Model 1886.

Mechanical function: Similar to that of Model 1886 except box magazine instead of tubular; designed for high power cartridges.

Below: Model 1895 First Model Flatside lever action rifle in .30 Army caliber. Winchester made unsuccessful efforts to sell this model to the U.S. Army, but bolt action Mauser type rifles were adopted by most countries including the U.S.

Above: Winchester shotguns, top to bottom Model 1887 lever action; the best-selling slide-action Model 1897; the semiautomatic Model 1911, designed by T.C. Johnson; and the pump action Model 12, most successful shotgun of all Winchester pumps.

succeeded by the Model 1897, which was produced up to 1957. Production was over 1,000,000. To quote from *Flayderman's Guide to Antique American Firearms*, 7th Edition, "the new gun achieved instant popularity, and became the best selling slide action shotgun on the market. No other exposed hammer gun of its type has approached its success and fame. A number of Model 97s are still in field use at this writing."

The Model 1897 Slide Action was made in 12 and 16 gauge with barrel lengths 28 inches and 30 inches. There were three grades, marked on the barrel: Standard, Trap, and Pigeon, with Pigeon being the highest.

The short-barreled riot gun configuration proved to be extremely popular with police departments all over the United States, and in fact with variations is still in use. It was designed for crowd control and also use at short range, and

there are stories of perpetrators throwing down their weapons just from hearing the sound of the shotgun slide being cocked. Also, some 20,000 were used purchased by the Army for use as a trench gun in World War I. The Germans regarded this as barbaric, and at one point threatened to execute any Americans caught with this weapon in their possession (despite the fact that it was the German Army which initiated the use of poison gas).

Winchester missed a further major opportunity in the shotgun field and also lost its valuable relationship with John Browning in 1902, when it turned down Browning's invention of the automatic shotgun, and Browning took it to Fabrique Nationale (FN) in Belgium. Ultimately, this has led now to the Winchester company being owned by FN's parent, GIAT.

This dramatic story begins in 1889, when John Browning had the inspiration of developing a gun which would keep firing automatically once the trigger was pulled, using the power of the gas emitted at the muzzle. His son relates, in

John Browning, American Gunmaker, that the idea came to John at a shooting range in Ogden, when he noticed a clump of grass moving in front of the shooter, blown by muzzle blast. Browning's first crude device to use this power was in the form of a circular plate or "flapper" with a hole in the middle, attached to the muzzle, and also attached to a rod extending back to the lever working the gun's action. Later he substituted a gas port in the barrel near the muzzle. His first sale was of a machine gun, to Colt's (which was already manufacturing the Gatling hand-cranked machine gun). The Colt's-produced weapon was the forerunner of the Browning machine guns used in both World Wars I and II.

After a detour into pistol design, where he invented recoil as well as gas operated mechanisms and eventually the .45 caliber Colt Model 1911 and the .32 caliber Belgian Browning, John concentrated on developing an automatic shotgun. After much effort he sent this to Winchester, which patented it for Browning but then refused to produce it. The reason was either that Browning asked for a royalty arrangement for the first time, or that Winchester (T. G. Bennett) did not want to undertake the cost of development. Browning immediately went to Remington but its president, Marcellus Hartley, died of a heart attack on the morning of the day Browning had his appointment. This led to Browning setting sail for FN in Belgium for which he had already designed his .32 caliber automatic pistol. FN had great success in the sale of the automatic shotgun, also licensing the gun to Remington. Browning also set up his own company, Browning Arms, which is now part of the FN-GIAT family.

It took nine years for Winchester to develop a new semi-automatic shotgun design not covered by the Browning patents. A series of additional models have followed, but none as successful as the Browning-designed automatic shotgun of which over 5,000,000 have been made, by companies other than Winchester.

Browning also adapted his automatic gas operation to the Browning Automatic Rifle (BAR), used as a light machine gun. Ironically, Winchester received an order for some 46,000 BAR's for the Army at the end of World War I. The BAR was used extensively in World War II and the Korean War, but not then made by Winchester.

Model 1890 .22 slide action rifle

Many readers will remember this handsome little .22 rifle used in shooting galleries at amusement parks. Browning later told his son the story of how he stopped at a shooting gallery on the street after leaving his breakup meeting with T. G. Bennett at the Winchester headquarters, and upset the proprietor by consistently hitting the bullseye and qualifying for round after round of free cartridges (he more than paid for these when he finished). Invented by John Browning and his brother Matt, the rifle became the best selling item in the

Winchester line.

The rifle replaced the heavier .22 Model 1873, which had not been popular. Colt's brought out its .22 caliber slide action Lightning rifle in 1887, but the Browning design was superior and Colt's rifle was not a serious competitor.

Winchester used another of Browning's brilliant inventions to produce a simpler, lower priced .22 rifle, the Model 1900. Selling for only $5, it was a partial bolt action rifle in that the bolt handle opened and closed the chamber, but cocking was done by hand by pulling a knob at the rear of the bolt. It had an 18 inch round barrel only, a straight grip stock, and no buttplate; gumwood was used for the stock. Upgrading, including providing a buttplate, was done in 1902. Eventual sales of this rifle and additional modifications were over 1,000,000. The rifle was promoted by Winchester not only because of its own 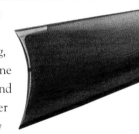 sales volume but on the theory, as expressed to its dealers, that a child who first uses a Winchester .22 rifle would eventually become a customer for a Winchester centerfire rifle or shotgun.

T. G. Bennett himself became the inventor of a .22 caliber rifle, the Thumb Trigger Model of 1904. It had the same simple bolt handle and cocking system as the Model 1900, but the "trigger" consisted of a button on top of the stock behind the receiver. It was advertised as an aid to accurate shooting, since the shooter would not tend to pull the gun to the side as would be the case with the conventional trigger. The rifle retailed for only $3.50, but was not particularly popular; most of the 59,000 produced were shipped to Australia.

Below: Model 1897 shotgun, the World War I "Trench Gun," also used as a police riot gun (National Firearms Museum Collection, photo by NRA staff).

The first semi-automatic rifle

Winchester had another talented designer who came to the fore after the breakup with Browning, Thomas C. Johnson. He was the chief designer for the company from 1907 to approximately 1931. Among his first developments was a semiautomatic or self-loading rifle, the first to be commercially manufactured in the United States. This was recoil operated or blowback, with the amount of the recoil controlled by attaching a weight to the bolt. It was first produced in .22 caliber as the Model 1903, and had an enthusiastic reception. Total production to 1923 was 126,211. Additional models were developed and produced up to the Model 1910, in calibers up to .401 Winchester.

Above: Model 1890 .22 Short caliber slide action rifle, the popular gallery gun, in deluxe configuration with 24 inch octagonal barrel and Winchester A5 telescopic scope, evidently used for target shooting or very small game.

Below: Deluxe Third Model 1890 slide action rifle in .22 Long Rifle caliber, with 24 inch octagonal barrel marked "stainless steel." Also fitted with folding tang disc sight and sling swivels. Shotgun style butt with serrated cap.

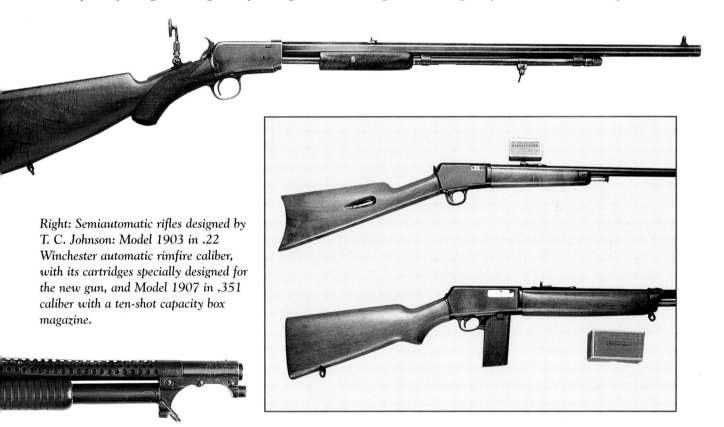

Right: Semiautomatic rifles designed by T. C. Johnson: Model 1903 in .22 Winchester automatic rimfire caliber, with its cartridges specially designed for the new gun, and Model 1907 in .351 caliber with a ten-shot capacity box magazine.

MODEL 1890 .22 SLIDE ACTION RIFLE

Type: Multi-shot slide action rifle with magazine tube under the barrel.

Made: 1890-1932.

Variations: First model, serial to about 15521, not takedown, casehardened frame. Second model includes takedown type, serial to 326615, frame usually not casehardened. Third model also includes takedown, serial to end of production, locking lugs visible in notch on top of each side of frame.

Quantity: Approximately 849,000.

Caliber: .22 Short, Long, and Long Rifle.

Barrel length: 22 inches, octagonal.

Markings: Winchester name and address, patent dates, model and caliber markings on the barrel; serial numbered on the lower tang. Blued finish except where casehardened.

THE WINCHESTER RIFLES OF THEODORE ROOSEVELT

Theodore Roosevelt was a human dynamo. He was the 26th and youngest President of the United States (at age 42, serving from 1901 to 1909). He was an avid hunter, a Nobel Prize winner, a wildlife conservationist, a war hero, a life member of the National Rifle Association, an author of 39 books, a father of six, and the most gun-savvy man ever to occupy the White House. When it came to gun knowledge or shooting skill, no chief executive, now or then, was his peer.

When it came to firearms he wrote a number of times that his favorite was the Winchester: "The Winchester stocked and sighted to suit myself is by all odds the best weapon I ever had, and I now use it almost exclusively..." (in *Hunting Trips of a Ranchman*).

From his first Winchester, a Model 1876 he ordered when he was 22 years old, to his favorite Model 1895, last used on a river exploration just scant years before his death at the age of 60, Roosevelt's Winchesters are now legend and priceless pieces of Americana.

Roosevelt's poor eyesight may have been a mitigating factor in his fondness for the arms of the Winchester Repeating Arms Company. He was

Above: "Teddy" Roosevelt posed in dude-like Western garb of fringed buckskin, big game hunting rifle at the ready. TR was caught up with the romance of the Old West after buying a ranch in the Dakota Badlands.

quoted as saying that he "didn't know how to shoot well, but I know how to shoot often." No gun of the period shot more often or as reliably as did the Winchester. Capable of holding as many as 16 cartridges in some models, the predecessor of the first Winchester, the Henry, was called "that infernal rifle you could load on Sunday and shoot all week." Confederate soldiers who had the misfortune of finding themselves on the receiving end also referred to it as "a horizontal shot tower."

Roosevelt no doubt enjoyed the capability of having plenty of ammunition in the gun as well as having a firearm that could easily bring each successive round into battery with effortless ease and remarkable reliability. To a man whose shooting skill was severely hampered by his eyesight,

(nearsightedness and later blindness in one eye), the fact that a Winchester could be sighted and fired, and fired again without having to remove the gun from his shoulder would have been a welcome feature for this "Bull Moose."

He special ordered his first Winchesters in the late summer of 1881, possibly to celebrate the publication of his second book, *The Naval War of 1812*. He ordered a pair of consecutively numbered Model 1876s. These guns would be similar in composition to nearly every one of the next 20 Winchesters that he ordered. When he wrote "stocked and sighted to suit me," he meant that the gun barrels should be half-round, half-octagon, pistol-gripped, deluxe checkered wood, sometimes factory engraved, case hardened, plain

This chapter has been contributed by Philip Schreier, Curator of Programs, National Firearms Museum of the National Rifle Association.

Above: One of Theodore Roosevelt's special order Model 1876 carbines. Note half-round, half-octagon barrel, pistol grip, deluxe checkered wood, case hardened receiver, half-magazine, sling swivels, and shotgun butt.

trigger, half-magazine, shotgun butt, and special sights. Generally, enough special order features were desired by TR to cause the price of the gun to double!

In the summer of 1883, TR was hit with another bout of wanderlust that directed his daydreams to the plains of the Wild West. As a New York Assemblyman, he was constantly aware of land schemes and speculators who promised riches for small investments. His father had passed away in 1878 providing him with a not insignificant financial foundation and, following a fortuitous meeting with a land promoter, he decided to check out the Dakota Badlands along the Little Missouri River.

His Winchesters caught the attention of everyone who saw them and they marveled at the exquisite nature of the engraving and checkering. William Dantz, who remembered meeting Roosevelt, was so impressed by one Winchester that he mistook it for the exceedingly rare 1 of 1000 model (TR never did own a 1 of 1000 model).

To those who had grown up on the plains, TR was the epitome of an eastern dude. Dressed in a fringed and embroidered shirt and buckskin pants with a wide-brimmed Boss-of-the-Plains Stetson, he looked the part that every dime novelist depicted of the hapless greenhorn.

Though his trip diary mentions nothing of the two deluxe Winchesters in his personal inventory, TR managed in 16 days to bag one bison, a black-tailed buck, assorted rabbits, grouse, teal, and other such wildlife all taken with a Sharps .45 caliber 1874 Sporting rifle or a 10-gauge double-barreled shotgun that had been a gift from his brother Elliott. He was so impressed with his guide Joe Ferris and the territory that he had traveled that he promptly purchased a sizeable ranch and made Ferris a foreman along with fellow guide William Merrifield.

Roosevelt returned east to run for re-election and await the expected birth of his first child who was due in mid-February of 1884. As the winter passed in New York, the re-elected assemblyman began to plan a grizzly bear hunt for his next trip to the Badlands and purchased a second ranch called the Elkhorn, not far from his Maltese Cross ranch purchased the year before.

Right: Roosevelt on a Western bear hunt, with a Winchester Model 1894 rifle with two-third magazine and deluxe cheekpiece stick. Some of TR's hunting guides and neighbors in the Dakotas joined his "Rough Riders" in the Spanish-American War.

On Valentine's Day, 1884, TR received a wire while on the floor of the New York State House in Albany. He rushed home to New York City to find that his wife had delivered a healthy baby girl, named Alice Lee after her mother. However the heartfelt joy of a first child was quickly diminished as first TR's mother and then his wife both died within hours of each other in the same house. Devastated and heartbroken, TR sought to find solace in the Badlands of the Wild West.

Scheduled to begin his second expedition exactly one year after his first one had begun, TR ordered two more Winchesters, an 1873 in .32-20 and another 1876 in .45-75 (the previous two had been in .50-95). Roosevelt had pretty much decided to lose himself in the Dakota Territory and make a go of being a rancher. Some would say that in his depressed state of mind he might have had a death wish that emboldened him and made him somewhat fearless, since the consequences of rash behavior mattered little to him.

Once, while in a saloon, a cowhand strode in and, seeing the dude'ed up easterner with his glasses prominently affixed to his nose, said, "Four eyes is buyin," and proceeded to claim a drink at Roosevelt's expense. TR quietly withdrew to a

Above: Theodore Roosevelt in his colonel's uniform in the field in the Spanish-American War, 1898. He helped recruit the 1st US Cavalry Regiment that became known as Roosevelt's "Rough Riders."

Above: Famous photo of Roosevelt and his triumphant troopers, after the capture of Kettle and San Juan Hills. This heroic feat helped propel Roosevelt into the presidency.

table nearest the stove in hopes that the bravado of the cowboy might soon be forgotten, but no such luck. The cowboy, drawn pistols in hand, sauntered up to the diminutive TR (he was only 5 feet 9 inches and at this time weighed about 155 pounds) and demanded Roosevelt confirm that he was indeed buying the house drinks. Roosevelt rose from his chair and faced the cowboy whose revolvers very nearly touched against the torso of TR. He struck hard and quick with a right, left, and then another right hand punch that dropped the blowhard to the floor like a sack of fresh chips.

It was possibly during this trip that TR made a present of one of those first new Winchesters that he had bought in 1881. He had a special gold plate (a motif that he would use repeatedly) engraved and mounted on the butt with an inscription to William Merrifield and it carried the brand of the Maltese Cross ranch. He also lost no time in having a number of images of his likeness made showing off both his new rifle and Tiffany silver knife as well as his entire "Western ensemble" that included another set of buckskins and a fur hat!

This time, the hunting was after Roosevelt's first taste of dangerous game, a grizzly bear. During the hunt, TR and Merrifield came upon the king of North American beasts. He recounted to his sister in a letter:

"I shall not soon forget the first (grizzly) I killed. We had found where he had been feeding on the carcass of an elk; and followed his trail to a dense pine forest, fairly choked with fallen timber. While noiselessly and slowly threading our way through the thickest part of it I saw Merrifield, who was directly ahead of me, sink suddenly to his knees and turn half around, his face fairly ablaze with excitement. Cocking my rifle and stepping quickly forward, I found myself face to face with the great bear, who was less than twenty five feet off – not eight steps. He had been roused from his sleep by our approach; he sat up in his lair, and turned his huge head slowly towards us. At that distance and in such a place it was very necessary to kill or disable him at the first fire; doubtless my face was pretty white, but the blue barrel was as steady as a rock as I glanced along it until I could see the top of the bead fairly between his two sinister looking eyes; as I pulled the trigger I jumped aside out of the smoke, to be ready if he charged; but it was needless, for the great brute was struggling in the death agony, and as you will see when I bring home his skin, the bullet hole in his skull was as exactly between his eyes as if I had measured the distance with a carpenters rule. This bear was nearly nine feet long and weighed over a thousand pounds."

Right: The "Rough Riders" coming into camp. The troops were issued bolt action Krag carbines which the Army had adopted over the Winchester lever action, to Winchester's disappointment.

The trip lasted seven weeks, the longest hunting expedition mounted by Roosevelt until his African safari of 1909-1910.

A review of various articles and books, most notably R. L. Wilson's *Theodore Roosevelt – Outdoorsman*, confirms that TR had at least 20 Winchester rifles in his collection. By far, it was the gun for Roosevelt. When it came to presenting a gift to an admired associate or hunting companion, Roosevelt was quick to share his affection for Winchesters with those he honored by his generosity. The Metcalf brothers of Mississippi, who had provided the president with a bear hunt in 1902, a hunt that begat the legend of the Teddy Bear, were each presented with identical Winchester Model 1886s exactly like the president's own model. Another 1886 was also a gift to guide Holt Collier.

Possibly one of the finest and most historic gifts made by Roosevelt was a Winchester Model 1895, serial number 23576. As with most of TR's Winchesters, this rifle was embellished with a gold plate, and was inscribed "To Leonard Wood, Governor of Cuba, 12-29-99 from TR." At the time of the rifle's presentation, TR was governor of New York and General Leonard Wood had just accepted the stewardship of the island of Cuba as her governor. Wood was a career Army officer and Medal of Honor winner who in May of 1898 had accepted command of the 1st US Volunteer Cavalry and was somewhat chagrined to find that his second in command was the former Assistant Secretary of the Navy, Theodore Roosevelt. However, during training in San Antonio and in combat in

Cuba, TR proved himself to be an efficient soldier and inspiring leader. When he was called to accept a promotion at the divisional level, Wood felt confident that Roosevelt could handle the command of the unit that was now affectionately known as Roosevelt's Rough Riders by the press.

By nightfall of July 1, 1898, Roosevelt had led his men directly into the pages of the history books with their gallant charge up Kettle and San Juan Hills. Roosevelt's charge won him a place on McKinley's re-election ticket as vice-president, as well as a recommendation for the Medal of Honor. He gave his former commander an exquisite 1895 rifle as a token of his esteem at a period of time when both men were governors.

Whenever Winchester introduced a new model,

Right: Roosevelt and party, including son Kermit on his right, with Cape Buffalo heads, on his extended African safari of 1909-1910. Kermit holds a large caliber Model 1895 Winchester hunting rifle.

Left: Crates of Winchester rifles and ammunition packaged for delivery to the S.S. Hamburg in New York in 1909 for Roosevelt's safari. The total force for this well equipped expedition numbered 200 men.

his trip, TR's personal secretary William Loeb sent the following letter to Winchester:

To: The Winchester Repeating Arms Company
From: William Loeb, Jr., Secretary to the President.
Date: July 16, 1908

Gentlemen:
The president is going to Africa...He probably has all the rifles he needs but his son has not. Before deciding what he will buy, the president would like to see your catalog... Will you send your catalog to the President at Oyster Bay...?
Signed: Loeb

Roosevelt was quick to put it through its paces. He acquired an 1894 similar to all his other rifles in extras and embellishments and used it on an antelope hunt. His "little .30" as he called it, was able to knock down a good-sized antelope at a distance of over 180 yards. After witnessing the fantastic shot and the irrefutable and immediate results, TR's guide said that the gun was just "aces" in his book! TR also used a model 94 outfitted with a Maxim silencer at his Long Island home, "Sagamore Hill," so as not to disturb neighbors when some varmints were in need of culling.

Roosevelt's deeds with his Winchesters are certainly the stuff of legend. It would be difficult to find a more colorful figure so strongly linked to something that is now, and in no small measure due to his patronage, considered a household word and so instantly recognizable. Once while on a hunting trip he led in the capture of three river boat thieves, with an 1876 Winchester at the ready; another time while riding the boundary of his ranch he was set upon by a band of restless members of the Sioux tribe. One clear view of his Winchester across the saddle and they soon scattered. He would have been photographed holding a Winchester 1895 carbine atop San Juan Hill during the Spanish-American War had he not given it to another trooper in his unit who was without a rifle at the time.

A prolific writer, Roosevelt authored hundreds of magazine articles and six books about his hunting adventures. When it came to Winchesters he heaped praise upon them generously. His biggest and best publicized hunting expedition was the one he made to Africa with son Kermit in 1909-1910. Prior to the public announcement of

Such a simple letter started a chain of events that resulted in dozens of exchanges via wire and mail over the next year concerning the rifles and equipment needed for the great expedition to the sub-continent. Far from just wanting a few rifles for Kermit to have along on the safari, Roosevelt ended up having 15 wooden crates full of Winchester rifles, ammunition, spare parts, and equipment for his expedition shipped by Winchester to his waiting steamer. Of the rifles, he choose the 1895 lever action in .30-40 US as well as in .405 WCF to be the highlighted arms of the trip.

The 1895 Winchester was a departure from TR's standard taste in rifles. Designed by John Browning, the 1895 was the first Winchester to accept the new smokeless "hi-powered" rounds that were now revolutionizing the shooting world. With a tubular magazine being not only impracticable but dangerous as well when loaded with spitzer bullets, Browning developed a rifle action that still allowed the user to get off quick successive shots that would could hit harder and farther away with the new "hi-power" rounds. Roosevelt had seen the awesome effect smokeless cartridges had on battlefield tactics in Cuba in 1898 when his men were subject to withering fire from

Spanish forces armed with the new Mausers that used the smokeless powder. For Roosevelt, the combination of the fast working lever action and the power the new sporting cartridges packed made Winchester's 1895 the perfect rifle.

Introduced in 1904, the .405 cartridge was the most powerful round ever developed for a Winchester lever action rifle. Roosevelt had to have not one, not two, but three 1895s in .405 and the firearm proved very effective on almost every sort of game in Africa. The big, 300-grain bullet was a hard hitter with an initial muzzle velocity of over 2,230 feet per second.

In perhaps the best presidential endorsement of any product ever, Roosevelt wrote in *Scribners Magazine:* "The Winchester .405 is, at least for me personally, the medicine gun for lions." He created a sensation for the gun that lasts to this day. The .405 was discontinued in 1936. However, rifles chambered in "Teddies" caliber continue to bring a high premium over examples that are chambered in a round still readily available. In the year 2000, Winchester announced the re-introduction of the Browning 1895 in .405 caliber. The spirit of "Big Medicine" is still alive and well.

Aside from those rifles given as presents to guides and friends, most of Roosevelt's firearms are available for public viewing at a number of institutions across America.

Theodore Roosevelt's Birthplace Home, No. 28 East 20th St, New York City and his family home, "Sagamore Hill" on Long Island, both display a number of firearms associated with his military and sporting careers. The Buffalo Bill Historical Center, the Gene Autry Museum of Western Heritage, and the NRA's National Firearms Museum all have numerous firearms on public view that figure prominently in TR's writings as well as his contemporary photographs.

In recognition of Winchester's debt to Theodore Roosevelt and in celebration of his unique roles as the manufacturer's most historic patron and one of the world's greatest conservationist of wildlife and natural resources, the company issued the Theodore Roosevelt Commemorative, in 1969. The impressive total of 52,386 rifles and carbines would have been greater but for union problems at the time of issue.

To Winchester enthusiasts, and to all gun and hunting devotees, TR will ever be a heroic figure – the perfect example of the responsible hunter, sportsman, and shooter. He was an authentic statesman who knew, understood, and loved firearms. TR comprehended what firearms represent not only to a free society, but to the future of conservation and the sustained use of natural resources.

Below: Theodore Roosevelt and some of the safari members with a trophy elephant. Judging by the military uniform in the background, the expedition had good security.

Below: Famous photo of TR with his trophy rhinoceros, which he shot with the large caliber lever action Winchester he is holding, evidently a Model 1895. Present day safaris emphasize the camera over the rifle!

WINCHESTERS IN THE WORLD WARS

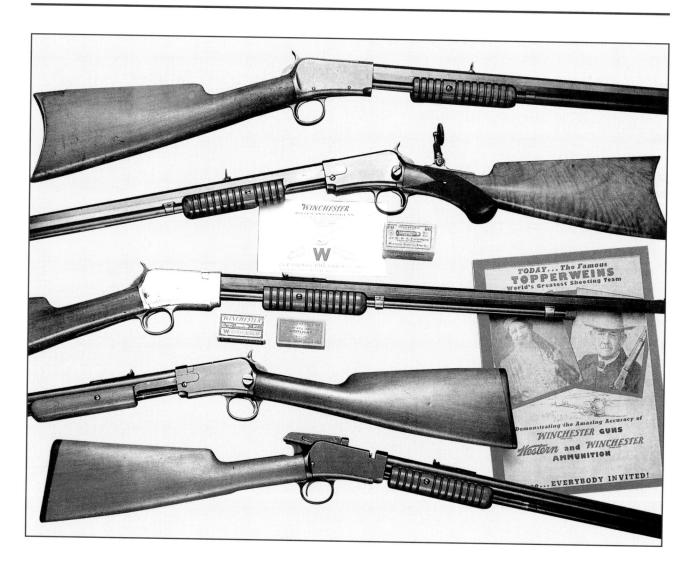

The Winchester company experienced strong growth from 1890 to 1914. Production reached an average of some 300,000 firearms per year, up by a factor of five, while employment, at over 6,000, was up by a factor of four. However, additional arms companies had come into the field, including Savage and Stevens, and Remington expanded after Winchester sold its interest in that company in 1896, so Winchester's share of the industry stayed about the same.

It is interesting to consider Winchester's sales promotion efforts during this period. The company employed "missionaries" as well as salesmen, to publicize the company with dealers and at shooting clubs and exhibitions. After 1903 Winchester also employed shooters who would go in competitions and put on exhibitions, notably the famous Adolph (Ad) Topperwein and his wife, Elizabeth, called "Plinky." She had previously worked in the Winchester ammunition loading room and, while learning to shoot, would say, "Throw up another one and I'll plink it." The company struggled to keep store chains and mail order houses from discounting its products, and had a long battle

Above: Model 1890 (top three) and Model 1906 (bottom two) .22 caliber slide action rifles. These had great popularity, both in shooting galleries and with younger American shooters.

with Sears, Roebuck over this issue.

In 1914 this situation of relative stability abruptly changed, from the company's short range point of view for the better. War was declared among the European powers shortly after the assassination of Archduke Franz Ferdinand of Austria and his wife Sophie, in Sarajevo, the capital of Bosnia, then an Austrian province. The assassin was a young Serbian fanatic named Gavrilo Princip.

A tragic series of blunders led to the actual outbreak of war only a month later. The Austrian Foreign Minister was intent on punishing Serbia, not realizing that Russia was obligated to support that small nation. The German Kaiser had no objection to Austria declaring war on Serbia, which it did. Russia began to mobilize, Germany called on her to stop, and then declared war. France and England were bound by an alliance with Russia, and the Germans moved into neutral Belgium to attack France. In that terrible August, almost six million men went into battle: Germany with two million, Austria with 500,000, France and England with 1,700,000, and Russia with 1,400,000. Eventually, before the end of World War I, there were 65 million men under arms.

The rifle was the "queen of battle" for the infantrymen who made up the bulk of the armed forces. It was inevitable that the American arms industry would be called on by the Allies. Although America was officially neutral and there was considerable pro-German sympathy in the United States, there never seems to have been a consideration of selling to the Central Powers, and this would have been difficult with the British blockade of the European continent, in any event.

Winchester's Allied war contracts were all negotiated by J. P. Morgan and Company, the premier American investment banker, with offices in New York and London. Winchester's rifle production in the United States entailed 246,000 Enfield bolt action repeating rifles in .303 caliber for the British, and 293,000 Winchester Model 1895 muskets in 7.62mm caliber for the Russians. There were also large ammunition orders, such as for 174 million cartridges for the Russians.

The contracts were negotiated on a fixed fee basis not allowing for increased costs in materials and labor, and did not turn out to be profitable. Also, Winchester was obliged to undertake a massive building construction program in order to add the necessary capacity, requiring a large loan, from J. P. Morgan and Kidder, Peabody & Company of Boston. New buildings were interspersed among the old buildings, the intent being to carry out a plan previously developed for phasing out the older buildings for more modern quarters. Pictures of the plant as of 1916 show, as described by R. L. Wilson, a "veritable city." Employment rose from about 6,000 in 1914 to 11,500 in 1915 and 16,000 in 1916.

In the meantime, the United States moved in fits and starts toward entering the war. Although in France the war had turned into a stalemate of trench warfare, in May of 1916 the British scored a strategic victory at sea in the Battle of Jutland, driving the German fleet permanently back into port. This led the Germans to start a campaign of submarine warfare, which eventually involved sinking ships with Americans on board.

Also, in early 1916, the United States became

Above: Typical scene of horrific trench conditions in World War I. The soldier climbing to go "over the top" appears to be holding an Enfield rifle, which Winchester produced in great volume.

Above: Musket version of the Hotchkiss Model 1883 bolt action repeater, .45-70 caliber, rejected by the military.

Above: Lee Straight Pull bolt action rifle in .236 caliber, clip loaded; 15,000 sold to the Navy and saw use in the Spanish-American War

Below: Pattern 14 British Enfield bolt action rifle made for the British Government, and then later adapted for the U.S. in .30 caliber.

Above: Post-World War II M14 semi-automatic rifle in 7.62 mm NATO caliber. Note cartridges becoming smaller in this progression.

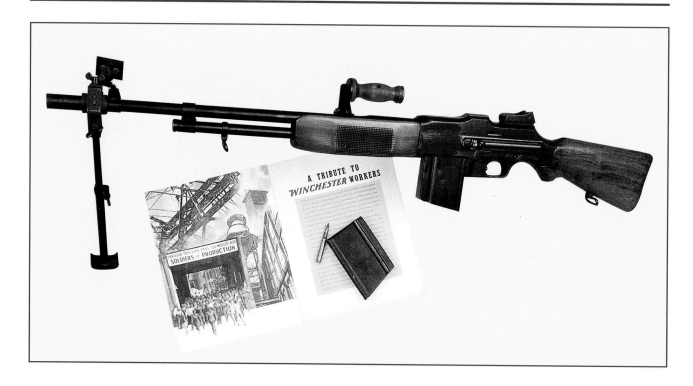

involved with Mexico, when Pancho Villa started a revolt against the Carranza administration, killing American citizens and even conducting a raid into New Mexico. The U.S. Army under "Black Jack" Pershing, with units called in from the National Guard, made an unsuccessful incursion into Mexico to find Villa, but the incident started a movement toward rearmament by the Americans, including universal conscription. On April 16, 1917, after the Germans declared unrestricted submarine warfare and American ships were sunk, and the notorious Zimmermann telegram to Mexico was intercepted proposing a German alliance with that country against the United States, Congress declared war on Germany.

Winchester had unused capacity following the completion of its contracts for the Allies, and two months before the United States declared war the company offered to turn its plant over to government production. The Army had adopted the Model 1903 Springfield rifle, based on a German Mauser design, ironically paying Mauser for the rights to produce it. However, the British Enfield was almost as good a rifle, and Winchester together with Remington proposed to use their already available machinery to produce Enfields modified to use the American .30-06 cartridge. The Ordnance Department agreed this time on the basis of cost plus 10 percent, and Winchester went into production of the rifle and the cartridge even before a formal contract was signed. Between 1917 and 1918 Winchester produced 465,980 of these rifles while Remington in Ilion, New York, produced 545,541, and Remington in Eddystone, Pennsylvania, produced 1,181,908.

Some three-fourths of the rifles used by the U.S. Army in World War I were the Enfield Model 1917, and only one-fourth were the Springfield Model 1903, contrary to popular impression. The movie starring Gary Cooper about Sergeant Alvin York, who single-handedly captured 132 Germans, shows him using a Springfield rifle, while he actually used an Enfield.

After the Allies smashed German Commander Ludendorff's final offensive with the help of the Americans, and Pershing's divisions began advancing steadily into Germany, the Germans surrendered in 1918 on what is still an American holiday, November 11. As in all the American wars, the Army and its suppliers faced virtually complete demobilization and the end of government orders.

The immediate problem was the repayment of the wartime loan from Kidder, Peabody. Its officers and investors agreed to keep Winchester going, but the funds that could not be repaid were converted into majority ownership shares for Kidder, Peabody, which also brought in officers of its own to help run the company. The aging T. G. Bennett and his son Winchester Bennett, whom T. G. had hoped would take over, were forced out. The new officers were John E. Otterson, who had actually been running the company as vice president since 1917, and Louis K. Liggett, who had set up the first national chain of pharmacies, Rexall, under the United Drug Company.

Having inherited a huge industrial complex with its wartime arms and ammunition business gone – the number of workers dropped from some 18,000 in 1918 to about 8,000 in 1919, and then down to about 4,000 in 1921 – the new owners and managers decided on an ambitious plan of beating swords into plowshares. They acquired a series of companies with products that could be manufactured in the New Haven plant, and also, following Liggett's example, started to establish a national chain of sporting goods and hardware stores. The list of products, advertised using the Winchester name and the slogan "As Good as the Gun," included such items as pocket knives and cutlery, hardware store tools, flashlights and batteries, ice and roller skates, and fishing rods and reels. Washing machines and refrigerators, sporting goods including Louisville Slugger bats, and paints and brushes were added later. There was a Winchester store at Broadway and 42nd Street in New York City. The Simmons Hardware Company, the largest national hardware wholesaler, strongly objected to the Winchester stores, which sold directly from the manufacturer, but ended up by joining Winchester in 1922 with a new Winchester-Simmons holding company.

The whole plan was too ambitious, and the only real returns were to Kidder, Peabody from the interest on their loans. In 1924 John Otterson was dropped as president and replaced by Liggett. Like the stock market during the Roaring Twenties, the company had become overextended. Even before the 1929 stock market crash, the Winchester

stores were sold, the partnership with Simmons was terminated, and the company largely reverted to producing arms and ammunition. As the Great Depression worsened after 1929, however, sales diminished to the point where the company went bankrupt and into receivership. That in itself did not turn out to be a misfortune: the company was bought at a receiver's sale by its major competitor in the ammunition field, the Western Cartridge Company of East Alton, Illinois. This company was owned by the Olin family which was experienced in the arms field and recognized the value of continuing Winchester's fine Design Department and keeping up the company's valuable patents. Also, they wisely kept Edwin Pugsley as general superintendent, with his key production personnel.

The Olin Corporation was originally formed in 1892 by Franklin W. Olin to make black powder for nearby coal mines, and also powder for shotgun loads. In 1898 it became the Western Cartridge Company, a major competitor of Winchester in ammunition manufacture, as discussed above. The company was always a leader in chemicals for gunpowder. In 1936 a new smokeless powder was invented by the company's Dr. Fred Olsen, which saw great use in World War II pistols and longarms and beyond, as "ball" powder. This is nitrocellulose with a small amount of nitroglycerin added, combined under water to form ball-shaped grains. Less expensive to manufacture than previous smokeless

Above: Enfield Pattern 13 – much modified up to WWI, made in US by Winchester, Eddystone and Remington. New rifle designated Pattern 14, which itself was modified for US Army, by whom it was designated Enfield 1917.

U.S. RIFLE, CALIBER .30, MODEL 1917 (ENFIELD)

Type: Bolt action rifle with five-shot clip-fed magazine.

Made: 1917-1918.

Variations: Made and marked at three manufacturing plants, Winchester at New Haven, Connecticut; Remington at Ilion, New York; and Remington at Eddystone, Pennsylvania. Name of manufacturer shown on top of receiver ring.

Quantity: By Winchester 465,980; by Remington at Ilion, 545,541; by Remington at Eddystone, 1,181,908.

Caliber: .30-06.

Barrel length: 26 inches.

Markings: U.S. MODEL 1917 (WINCHESTER or REMINGTON, ILION or EDDYSTONE), and serial number. Dark bluing on metal parts.

Mechanical function: Bolt action, cocking on closing; no cocking handle on the bolt. High profile shroud on rear sight, with a sliding peep aperture graduated to 1,600 yards, adjustable for elevation only. Similar to the British Enfield produced by Winchester in 1915 and 1916, except modified to use the rimless .30-06 cartridge instead of the rimmed .303 cartridge.

powders, ball powder continues to be used today (except for weapons used by the U.S. military, which found during the Vietnam War that it tended to swell when exposed to heat and moisture).

All during the 1920s and up to World War II, Winchester continued to produce its time-tested line of rifles such as the Model 1894 lever action rifle, and also continued to introduce new lines such as the Model 52 .22 target rifle and the Model 70 high power bolt action hunting rifle. As these are part of the story of Winchester up to the present day, these will be discussed in the next chapter.

New military orders were on the horizon during the 1920s and 1930s. The horrendous lessons of World War I had not been learned, and Hitler was allowed to rearm his Nazi Germany. The German Army moved into Poland on September 1, 1939, and World War II was on.

This time there was no immediate rush by the Allies to buy guns from the United States, since the U.S. Government had a declared policy of neutrality. President Franklin D. Roosevelt was widely criticized, a year after the European war began, in supplying 50 overage destroyers to England as "lend-lease," in Britain's darkest hour of its cities being attacked by the German Luftwaffe and its Atlantic supply line being almost severed by German submarines. There were apparently no shipments of smallarms from the United States; the author has an Enfield rifle made for the British by Savage and Stevens, marked U.S. Property, but the date is only 1942, after the United States entered the war. However,

Below: Winchester was the preeminent private manufacturer of the three major Army rifles from World War II through the early 1960s, the M1 Carbine, which it developed, the M1 Garand rifle, and the M14 semiautomatic rifle.

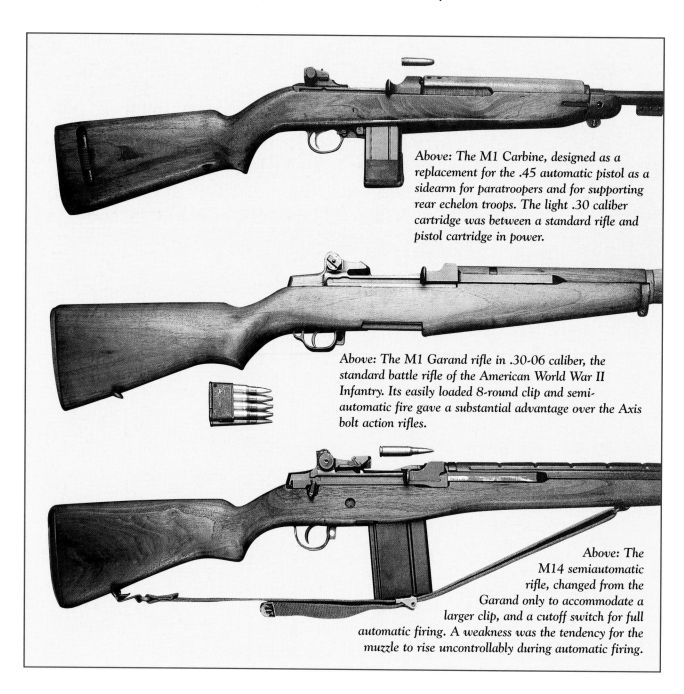

Above: The M1 Carbine, designed as a replacement for the .45 automatic pistol as a sidearm for paratroopers and for supporting rear echelon troops. The light .30 caliber cartridge was between a standard rifle and pistol cartridge in power.

Above: The M1 Garand rifle in .30-06 caliber, the standard battle rifle of the American World War II Infantry. Its easily loaded 8-round clip and semi-automatic fire gave a substantial advantage over the Axis bolt action rifles.

Above: The M14 semiautomatic rifle, changed from the Garand only to accommodate a larger clip, and a cutoff switch for full automatic firing. A weakness was the tendency for the muzzle to rise uncontrollably during automatic firing.

Above: Another view of the M1 Carbine, showing the side-mounted sling. The gun was also known in the Army as "new Winchester carbine, caliber .30."

Above: A World War II machine gun squad, carrying M1 carbines in their intended use for supporting troops.

Above: James Stewart, who played Carbine Williams in the film of the same name, poses with Williams and the carbine.

THE M1 CARBINE

Type: Semiautomatic light rifle with detachable box magazine, 15- or 30-round capacity. Also attachment provided to serve as rifle grenade launcher.

Made: 1941-1945; many were armory rebuilt after World War II.

Variations: Various changes made during World War II such as adjustable rear sight and barrel band with a bayonet lug. Some issued with folding metal stocks for airborne troops, called the M1A1. At the end of World War II, M2 model issued with adapter for full automatic. T3 model with infrared night vision scope used in the Korean War.

Quantity: 6,221,220, made by 10 contractors, Winchester, Inland Manufacturing Division of General Motors, Underwood-Elliott-Fisher, Rock-Ola Manufacturing, Quality Hardware Machinery, National Postal Meter, Irwin-Pedersen Arms, International Business Machines, Saginaw Steering Division of General Motors, and Standard Products. Winchester production, 828,059.

Caliber: .30, smaller than the .30-06, specially designed for the carbine.

Markings: U.S. M1 and name of manufacturer.

Mechanical function: Gas port located part way down the barrel, not at the muzzle, with a short stroke piston acting on the rod operating the action. Delay in rearward motion of the bolt by first rotating out its locked position allows dissipation of gas pressure. Weight less than five pounds.

by September 1940, with the fall of France, and Italy having entered the war on the German side, Roosevelt was able to induce Congress to pass the Selective Service Act and to approve raising an Army of 1,400,000 men, increasing aircraft production to 36,000 annually, and building a two-ocean Navy. The Olin Winchester Company was about to mobilize, dropping all civilian production as soon as the United States entered the war upon Japan's attack on Pearl Harbor, Hawaii, on December 7, 1941.

Although the United States did not begin large scale production of military smallarms until after entering the war, the Army and Winchester had been actively developing two new rifles which became mainstays during the war, and which were far in advance of the arms of other nations. Credit for the first, the M1 Garand infantry rifle, goes to the Springfield Armory and its designer John C. Garand, but Winchester was brought in to supplement Springfield for its production. The second, the M1 Carbine, was Winchester's own development, with its own designer David Marsh Williams.

The Army recognized the need for a self-loading or semiautomatic rifle immediately after World War I ("semiautomatic" is where the trigger is pulled for each shot, while the term "automatic," sometimes used interchangeably, is technically where the gun keeps firing as long as the trigger is depressed and until the ammunition is used up). There was a Board convened for this purpose, and a series of designs by Garand and others was considered until the Garand design was approved in 1936. It used the John Browning concept of the gas from the muzzle blast driving an operating rod to work the action, by means of a gas port under the barrel near the muzzle. It was a tremendous success during World War II, being described by General George S. Patton as "the greatest battle implement ever devised."

Winchester played a critical role in the production of the new rifle. In 1938 the company won an "educational contract" issued by the Army as preparation for private companies to supplement the Springfield Armory's capacity to produce the rifles when the need would arise. Winchester had to make one tool, one fixture, and one gauge for each component and then produce 500 rifles. An additional contract for 65,000 Garand rifles was received in 1939. From the beginning to the end of World War II, the company was the only private contractor to make the rifle, and turned out a total of 507,880.

Unlike the M1 rifle, the M1 Carbine was entirely a Winchester development. The company had been experimenting with a light rifle since 1930, when Jonathan E. Browning of the John Browning family patented a design for a civilian rifle which could be adapted for military use. In 1939, with the Jonathan Browning design still having problems, the company engaged David M. Williams, who had the new idea of the short stroke piston. The colorful story of Williams and his invention was later put into the movie "Carbine Williams," with James Stewart: Williams had whittled a model out of wood while serving time for murder in a North Carolina jail.

The Army had recognized the desirability of a small lightweight rifle since World War I, and in fact had conducted limited tests of other Winchester designs. However, when the war in Europe began and the German "Blitzkrieg" tactics emerged, the Army recognized a new need. War was no longer limited to front line troops in trenches, but the "rear echelon" soldiers could also suddenly become involved in combat. They would need arms less cumbersome than the M1 rifle but more effective than the Model 1911 pistol. Such a light rifle could also be carried by line officers, crew-served weapons teams, and other combat troops.

Designs were solicited and tests held by the Army during 1940. Winchester did not enter this competition, being totally occupied with producing the new M1 rifle. However, Winchester's Edwin Pugsley wrote Col. Rene R. Studler of the Ordnance Department about the progress Winchester was making with Williams's design, and Studler asked that a sample be made up using the light .30 caliber cartridge the Army had developed. This was done in only two weeks (over the objections of the volatile Williams, who reportedly threatened to shoot a co-worker who was pressing him to speed up his work). In October, 1941, the gun was adopted as being far ahead of all competitors.

The M1 Carbine was produced in unprecedented numbers during World War II, and was also used throughout the Korean War of 1950 to 1953, and even in the opening stages of the Vietnam War in 1964. The M1 Garand rifle continued to be produced by the Springfield Armory up to 1957, when it was replaced by the M14 rifle. This was based on the same system as the Garand, lightened somewhat and fitted with a 20-round box magazine and with full automatic capability, which, however, was not usable because with its .308 caliber cartridge the muzzle could not be held down during automatic fire ("became an anti-aircraft gun").

Winchester made over 350,500 of these starting in 1959 but, with excessive production costs, lost money. When the Colt AR-15 in .228 caliber was adopted by the Army as the M16, a modern design still being used, Winchester obtained a contract for 18,000 barrels. In the meantime the Western Cartridge division was a major ammunition supplier, including operating government arsenals.

Above: Standard M1 Carbine, as made by 10 contractors during World War II. The magazine shown has a 30-round capacity. The slot at the rear of the stock held an oil container, which also anchored the sling.

Below: Model M1 A1 Carbine with folding wire stock for use by airborne troops. These were landed on hostile battlefields either by parachute or by glider.

Above: Standard M1 Garand rifle, with military sling. Note stacking swivel near the muzzle. The earliest design had a "gas port" in the barrel, but later models used gas from the muzzle to work the operating rod under the barrel.

Above: M1A1 Carbine, made up to commemorate the Airborne services. Note the oiler bottle in the folding stock and the pistol grip.

Right: Same with pistol grip folded, illustrating how it could be used one handed. The weight of the standard carbine was only five pounds.

Left: M14 semiautomatic rifle with flash suppressor attached to the muzzle. This was the last model produced at the Springfield Armory, which closed in 1964 when the Army adopted the Colt AR15 automatic rifle in .223 caliber.

HUNTING AND SPORTING ARMS SINCE THE 1920S

Oliver Winchester's dream of government contracts came magnificently true in World Wars I and II, but led to loss of independence and repeated changes in ownership in the postwar slumps. However, development and sales of its civilian rifles and shotguns have remained impressively steady. A review of the major models listed in the Year 2000 Winchester catalog illustrates this point very clearly; all the company's best known lines are represented.

Below: Winchester .22 caliber rimfire rifles from the mid-1920s to late 1930s. From top, Models 56 and 57, with removable box magazines; Model 58, an economy continuation of the Model 1904; Model 59, only made in 1930; Model 60A with grooved fore-end; and Model 60A target model.

Before reviewing these models and their history, a brief explanation of the company's changes in ownership and present status is appropriate. It has been explained earlier how Olin Industries, with its Western Cartridge Company, took the bold and successful step of rescuing Winchester from bankruptcy in 1932, during the depths of the Great Depression. Then, as also described, the company stopped civilian production at the beginning of World War II and became a bulwark of the national defense.

After World War II, during which Winchester and Western Cartridge had grown temporarily to 61,000 employees, Olin Industries Inc. converted to peacetime operations by acquiring several other companies, and in 1954 merged with Mathieson Chemical to form the Olin-

Mathieson Corporation. This was a major conglomerate with products all the way from drugs and pharmaceuticals to rocket engines, with some 35,000 employees. The ammunition division expanded by developing plastic shotshells and a new gunpowder factory in Florida. Its Brass Group, manufacturing cartridge cases, was so advanced that it won the government contract to produce the cupronickel and copper sandwich metal to replace silver in the U.S. coinage.

Civilian firearms production at the Winchester plant in New Haven, Connecticut, was strong during the 1950s and 1960s, but there were damaging strikes in 1969 and 1979. Also, in the early 1950s, the City of New Haven sharply increased taxes on the Winchester plant. The Olins immediately decided to move as much as possible of their firearms operation out of New Haven, and demolished many of the factory buildings on the site. Then, in 1981, the Winchester Firearms Division was sold to a consortium formed by its management, under the name of the U.S. Repeating Arms Company.

One of the first initiatives of the new company was issuing the John Wayne Commemorative Model 94 carbine, with sales of over 51,000 arms. In 1987 44 percent of the stock was purchased by Fabrique Nationale (FN) of Belgium, who were already the owners of the Browning Arms Company with headquarters in Utah, the birthplace of the John Browning firearms inventions. In 1992, the parent of FN, GIAT, owned by the Wallonian Region of the Belgian Government, purchased the rest of the company's stock and had the Browning Arms Company take over management of Winchester.

The U.S. Repeating Arms Company now has a new, modern, 225,000 square foot plant with some 300 employees located on part of the original Winchester site. A commemorative book in the lobby includes pictures of the dedication ceremony of the new plant on October 14, 1994, attended by local notables and officials of GIAT, as the owners of FN. The company headquarters is shown as Morgan, Utah, the same address as Browning Arms. The Belgian flag now flies with the American flag over the Winchester plant.

From the current company catalog,

Above: One of the two last firearms made by Winchester-Olin before the company's breakup: a combination rifle and shotgun from about 1985, 12 gauge and .30-06 caliber. Engraved sideplates and telescopic sight.

Above: The other final Winchester-Olin model, the Grand Europe, double rifle in .30-06 caliber. The two models were made at the Olin-Kodensha works in limited quantities.

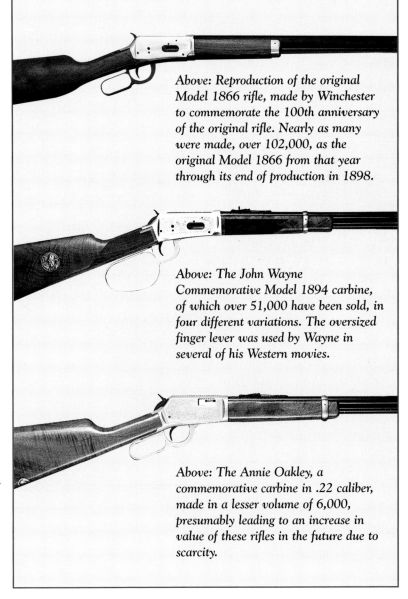

Above: Reproduction of the original Model 1866 rifle, made by Winchester to commemorate the 100th anniversary of the original rifle. Nearly as many were made, over 102,000, as the original Model 1866 from that year through its end of production in 1898.

Above: The John Wayne Commemorative Model 1894 carbine, of which over 51,000 have been sold, in four different variations. The oversized finger lever was used by Wayne in several of his Western movies.

Above: The Annie Oakley, a commemorative carbine in .22 caliber, made in a lesser volume of 6,000, presumably leading to an increase in value of these rifles in the future due to scarcity.

informal contacts with company employees, and a visit to the New Haven factory site, the author is convinced that the spirit of the sign proudly displayed at the entrance to the new factory is being carried on, supplemented by the new technology exemplified by the new plant: "Through These Gates Pass The Greatest Craftsmen Who Make The World Famous Winchester Firearms."

The Winchester rifles and shotguns are now being produced on a multinational basis: for example, barrels are made in the New Haven plant, engineering is done in Utah and Oregon, other metal parts are produced in Belgium, and stocks are made and guns assembled in Portugal. The New Haven plant also includes the Custom Shop. Classic reproductions are made in Japan. As many barrels are produced in the New Haven plant with modern technology, according to an employee's comment, as were produced when there was a huge 900,000 square foot factory complex on the site.

The new plant fits in well with the reuse that has been

Below: Sign at the entrance to the modern Winchester plant in New Haven, Connecticut, in what is now the Winchester Science Park. The plant occupies part of the site of the original huge Winchester complex.

made of the rest of the original Winchester property as the New Haven Science Park. A number of impressive new office, laboratory, and factory buildings have been built or have been adapted from older structures, appropriately complementing the Victorian homes of the former Winchester executives which still overlook the site.

The following are the principal lines of Winchester arms being produced as of the issuance of the Year 2000 catalog.

Model 1894 rifle

We may let the catalog speak for itself in describing the appeal of this popular rifle, which has had the largest production of any Winchester except for lower priced .22s:

"Why the Model 94 Winchester may be the world's perfect rifle. The reasons to shoot a Model 94 one hundred years ago are even more important today. Who can argue with over 100 years of dependable service? The 94 can take rough conditions – snow or rain, mud or dust – and keep working. Every caliber has a level of recoil you can handle, helping you to stay on target. It is compact and lightweight, able to go where you want to hunt . . . in the rugged, thick conditions where game likes to hide. It hunts the way you hunt today: fitting easily on an ATV rack or strapped onto a backpack or up in a cramped treestand or leading the way through an overgrown thicket. Few would dispute that more deer have fallen to the Winchester Model 94 than any other rifle in history."

The rifle is offered in a number of variations. The "Traditional" has the full 11-shot tubular magazine with a straight walnut stock, but can be upgraded as the "Legacy," with a pistol grip stock and special checkering. Compact versions are offered with shortened stocks and magazines, including the "Trapper." Calibers go up to "Big Bore," with the .444 Marlin cartridge. A "Black Shadow" composition stock is offered. Caliber .22 models are offered in full and compact size.

continued on page 90

Above: Winchester 8500 Special Trap over-and-under: 12 gauge, capacity 2, drop-down action, 30in barrel, weight 8.3lb. Bottom barrel is "ported" to vent some of the gases before they leave the muzzle.

Above: The Model 94 in .22 caliber, with takedown by a single screw. Available in either the traditional .22 Long Rifle or the longer, more powerful .22 Magnum (WMR).

Below: Illustration from the Winchester 2000 Catalog of a hunter using the Model 70 rifle with a custom stand. Telescopic sight suggests the game is at long range.

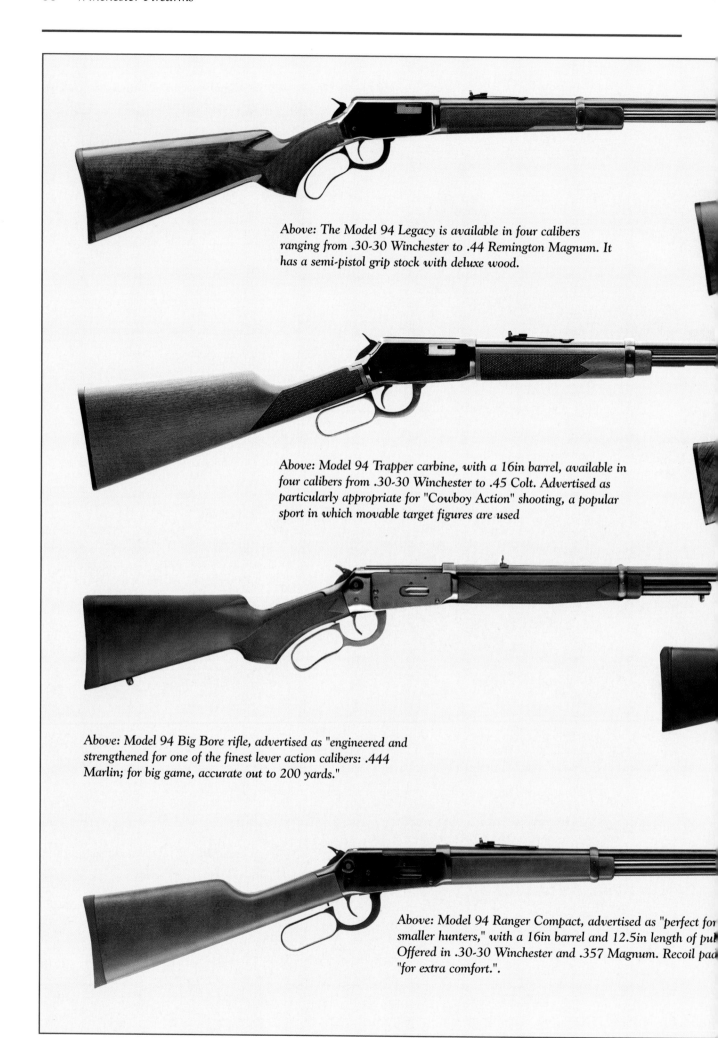

Above: The Model 94 Legacy is available in four calibers ranging from .30-30 Winchester to .44 Remington Magnum. It has a semi-pistol grip stock with deluxe wood.

Above: Model 94 Trapper carbine, with a 16in barrel, available in four calibers from .30-30 Winchester to .45 Colt. Advertised as particularly appropriate for "Cowboy Action" shooting, a popular sport in which movable target figures are used

Above: Model 94 Big Bore rifle, advertised as "engineered and strengthened for one of the finest lever action calibers: .444 Marlin; for big game, accurate out to 200 yards."

Above: Model 94 Ranger Compact, advertised as "perfect for smaller hunters," with a 16in barrel and 12.5in length of pull. Offered in .30-30 Winchester and .357 Magnum. Recoil pad "for extra comfort.".

Above: Model 94 Traditional, the most popular deer hunting rifle, made only in .30-30 Winchester caliber. From the Winchester 2000 catalog: "When you see a lever action afield, chances are it's the Traditional."

Above: Model 94 New Custom Limited Edition, in .44-40 caliber only. Advertised in Year 2000 catalog as a limited production of 75 rifles, it has a checkered stock, case-colored receiver, and satin blue octagonal barrel.

Below: Model 94 Black Shadow rifle, in .30-30 Winchester, .44 Magnum, and .444 Marlin calibers. Black composite synthetic stock with non-glare finish, and hunting-style stock dimensions with straight comb, "making scope use more effective."

Below: Right side view of Model 94 Custom Limited Edition rifle, made in .44-40 caliber. As advertised in the Year 2000 catalog, production is limited to 75 rifles.

Below: Left side view of the Custom Limited Edition Model 94 rifle. Advertised as having a spade checkered fancy stock and rich case-colored receiver and satin blue 24 inch match grade, full octagonal barrel.

Model 70 rifle

The top of Winchester's line of hunting rifles since it was introduced in 1936, the Model 70 is so well known as the "Rifleman's Rifle" that the expression is trademarked. Again it is appropriate to let the Year 2000 catalog describe the rifle:

> "*Famous because it works*. Few rifles have achieved the stature of the Model 70. No other rifle compares to its classic good looks, reputation for dependability and proven accuracy."

The predecessor of the Model 70 was the Model 54, which was made from 1925 to 1936. This was the first bolt action Winchester for smokeless powder centerfire, high-velocity, heavy-caliber cartridges. Production was over 50,000, in a variety of types in addition to the standard rifle, such as a carbine and heavy barrel target rifle. Calibers ranged from .22 Hornet to .30-06 Springfield.

The Model 70 incorporated a number of mechanical

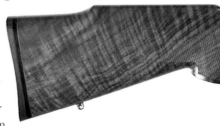

improvements (see box) plus, as described by R. L. Wilson, an overall more impressive styling and quality. The Year 2000 catalog shows a continuing improvement in the rifle's details. Among the mechanical features emphasized are the "massive claw extractor," which engages over one-fourth of the cartridge rim and maintains control in seating the cartridge ("controlled round feeding"). Also, there is a three-position safety which blocks the firing pin and allows opening the bolt with the safety on. Calibers offered go up to the .458 Winchester Magnum, and a wide range of types is listed such as the Classic Safari Express and Supergrade; the Compact, Featherweight, and

Below: The Model 54 bolt action rifle, the predecessor to the Model 70. Top, chambered in .220 Swift. Center, carbine configuration in .30-06 caliber. Bottom, target version in .22 Hornet, with Unertl scope and peep sights.

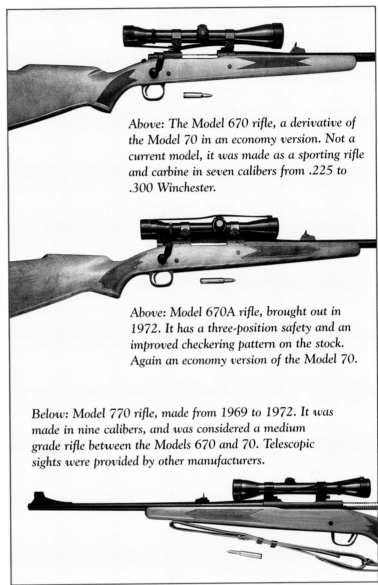

Above: The classic Model 70 bolt action rifle, made from 1936 to date, advertised and trademarked as "The Rifleman's Rifle, the standard for big game hunting worldwide." Some prefer the pre-1964 version, but present day quality is claimed to be as good.

Above: The Model 670 rifle, a derivative of the Model 70 in an economy version. Not a current model, it was made as a sporting rifle and carbine in seven calibers from .225 to .300 Winchester.

Above: Model 670A rifle, brought out in 1972. It has a three-position safety and an improved checkering pattern on the stock. Again an economy version of the Model 70.

Below: Model 770 rifle, made from 1969 to 1972. It was made in nine calibers, and was considered a medium grade rifle between the Models 670 and 70. Telescopic sights were provided by other manufacturers.

Ranger Compact; Stainless and Black Shadow; and New Coyote and Stealth. The rifle is known for its use for big game hunting in Africa, and Wilson comments that it is likely that more professional hunters and guides around the world rely on the Model 70 as their own rifle than any other.

There has been considerable controversy over the change in the Model 70 that took place in 1964. Pre-1964 rifles suddenly took on higher values. However, according to Robert W. Hunnicutt in *American Rifleman* magazine, when the Browning management took over Winchester in 1992, they brought in modern computer-controlled machinery that eliminated dozens of operations formerly carried out by human operators on individual machines; also, the new machines automatically monitor wear on cutters and replace them during machine operations. This has allowed returning to the pre-1964 claw extractor and controlled feed system. There no longer appears to be a concern over quality, but only over details such as the cone breech, which purposely has been eliminated.

continued on page 94

MODEL 70 HUNTING AND SPORTING RIFLE

Type: Bolt action rifle for hunting and target use, magazine three to six rounds.

Made: 1936 to date.

Variations: Significant changes made in 1947 and 1948. After 1964, some parts (not the frame) changed to precision castings instead of machined parts and lesser finish, but since 1992 there has been improved machinery and finish with added features.

Quantity: 1,500,000 reached in 1981.

Caliber: .22-223 to .476.

Barrel length: 22 to 26 inches.

Markings: Winchester or U.S. Repeating Arms Co., Model 70, caliber.

Mechanical function: Bolt action with handle turned up and pulled to the rear to eject used cartridge, then pushed forward to seat fresh cartridge. A series of special features are included such as claw extractor, field-strippable bolt, floorplate under the magazine attached to triggerguard, and three-position safety allowing opening the bolt with the safety on.

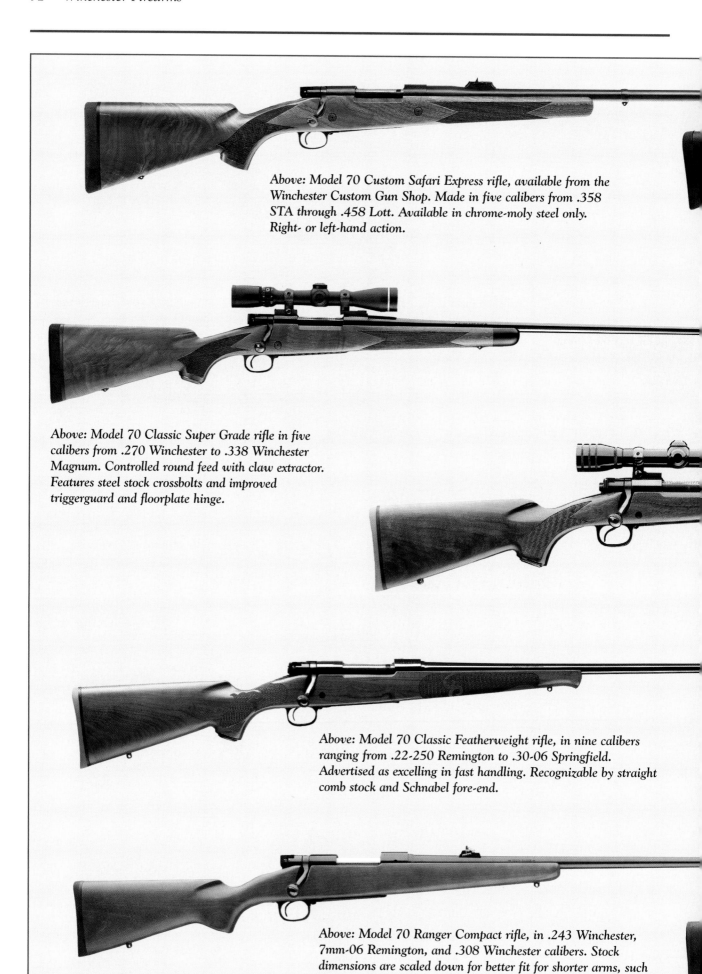

Above: Model 70 Custom Safari Express rifle, available from the Winchester Custom Gun Shop. Made in five calibers from .358 STA through .458 Lott. Available in chrome-moly steel only. Right- or left-hand action.

Above: Model 70 Classic Super Grade rifle in five calibers from .270 Winchester to .338 Winchester Magnum. Controlled round feed with claw extractor. Features steel stock crossbolts and improved triggerguard and floorplate hinge.

Above: Model 70 Classic Featherweight rifle, in nine calibers ranging from .22-250 Remington to .30-06 Springfield. Advertised as excelling in fast handling. Recognizable by straight comb stock and Schnabel fore-end.

Above: Model 70 Ranger Compact rifle, in .243 Winchester, 7mm-06 Remington, and .308 Winchester calibers. Stock dimensions are scaled down for better fit for shorter arms, such as for younger shooters. Push feed bolt.

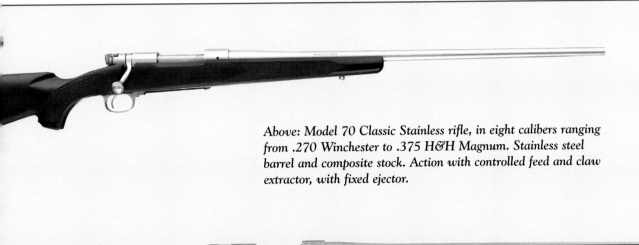

Above: Model 70 Classic Stainless rifle, in eight calibers ranging from .270 Winchester to .375 H&H Magnum. Stainless steel barrel and composite stock. Action with controlled feed and claw extractor, with fixed ejector.

Above: Model 70 Black Shadow rifle, in four calibers from .270 Winchester to .300 Winchester Magnum. Matte blued barrel and action, with black composite stock. Hinged floorplate and push feed bolt.

Above: Model 70 Classic Compact rifle, made in .243 Winchester, .308 Winchester, and 7mm-08 Remington calibers. Scaled down with shorter 20 inch barrel and shallower profile, advertised as an "ideal mountain rifle." Pre-1964 action with three position safety

Above: Model 70 New Coyote rifle made in .223 Remington, .22-250 Remington, and .243 Winchester calibers. Lightened barrel, designed for "carrying ease and pointability," with "the long range accuracy of a Varminter" (such as coyotes and chucks).

Above: Model 70 Stealth rifle, made in .223 Remington, .22-250 Remington, and .308 Winchester calibers. Heavier weight Varminter with heavy barrel stabilized by Kevlar-fiberglass-graphite stock and aluminum bedding block.

Shotguns

Winchester's largest selling shotgun over the years has been the slide action. This is represented to date by the Model 1300 Speed Pump, which was introduced in 1981. It has a three-shot capacity, two in the magazine and one in the chamber. Interestingly, this limitation on capacity was established by a U.S. Presidential Proclamation in 1935 for the conservation of migratory birds.

Operated by sliding the movable forearm in a trombone fashion, the Model 1300 is offered in a variety of styles for hunting and sporting use. Smoothbore barrels are used for bird shooting, rifled barrels are provided for deer hunting with slugs, and a combination of a smooth bore barrel and a rifled choke screwed onto the muzzle can be used for deer and turkey hunting. The shotgun is provided in 12 and 20 gauge: the higher number is the smaller size barrel; the numbers refer to solid lead balls that would just fit into the barrel, with the size determined by how many such balls would weigh one pound.

"Sporting" use means for trap, skeet, and sporting clays shooting done on specially constructed ranges. Trap shooting is done from stations arranged in an arc around a single ground level trap house from which breakable clay (now biodegradable composite) discs or "birds" are thrown up at different angles by a spring-loaded device. The sport originated by the use, up to 1866, of live pigeons released from a box. Skeet shooting uses a pair of trap houses, one high and the other low, at opposite ends of an arc of shooting stations. Sporting clays is a newer variation growing in popularity, where there is a greater variety of targets and types of release, even including bounding along the ground like a rabbit.

The early predecessor to the Model 1300 was the highly successful Model 1893, as described in a previous chapter, with its riot and trench gun variations. This was made up to 1979, while the military trench gun was made until 1945. Modifications to the basic shotgun were made in the form of the Model 1912, which had a production of over 2,000,000 up to 1980, and then the Model 1200.

Some of the special features of the present Model 1300 include a rotary bolt system as standard, optional Black Shadow and camouflage finish, and eight-shot shortened barrel Defender variations. Screw-on Winchokes, adopted in 1969, are available for all Winchester shotguns.

The Super X2 is Winchester's present version of a semiautomatic shotgun. This has a five-shot capacity, is in 12

continued on page 98

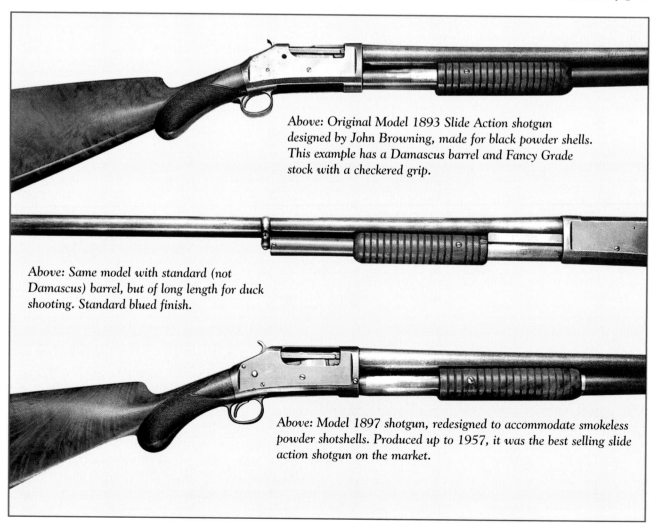

Above: Original Model 1893 Slide Action shotgun designed by John Browning, made for black powder shells. This example has a Damascus barrel and Fancy Grade stock with a checkered grip.

Above: Same model with standard (not Damascus) barrel, but of long length for duck shooting. Standard blued finish.

Above: Model 1897 shotgun, redesigned to accommodate smokeless powder shotshells. Produced up to 1957, it was the best selling slide action shotgun on the market.

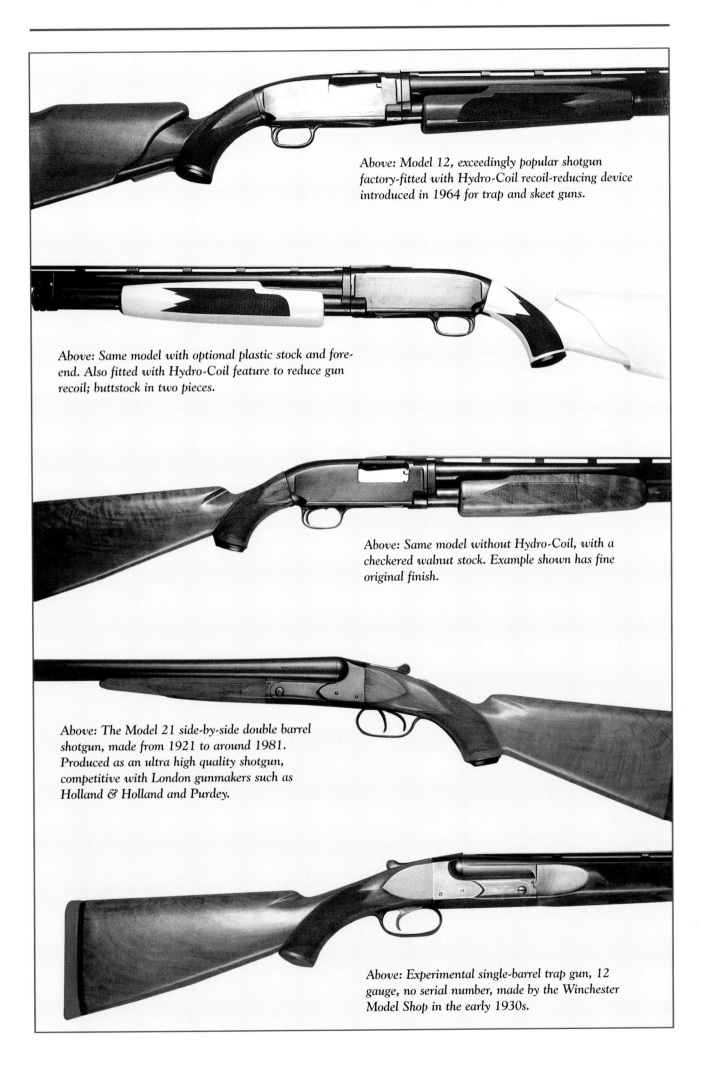

Above: Model 12, exceedingly popular shotgun factory-fitted with Hydro-Coil recoil-reducing device introduced in 1964 for trap and skeet guns.

Above: Same model with optional plastic stock and fore-end. Also fitted with Hydro-Coil feature to reduce gun recoil; buttstock in two pieces.

Above: Same model without Hydro-Coil, with a checkered walnut stock. Example shown has fine original finish.

Above: The Model 21 side-by-side double barrel shotgun, made from 1921 to around 1981. Produced as an ultra high quality shotgun, competitive with London gunmakers such as Holland & Holland and Purdey.

Above: Experimental single-barrel trap gun, 12 gauge, no serial number, made by the Winchester Model Shop in the early 1930s.

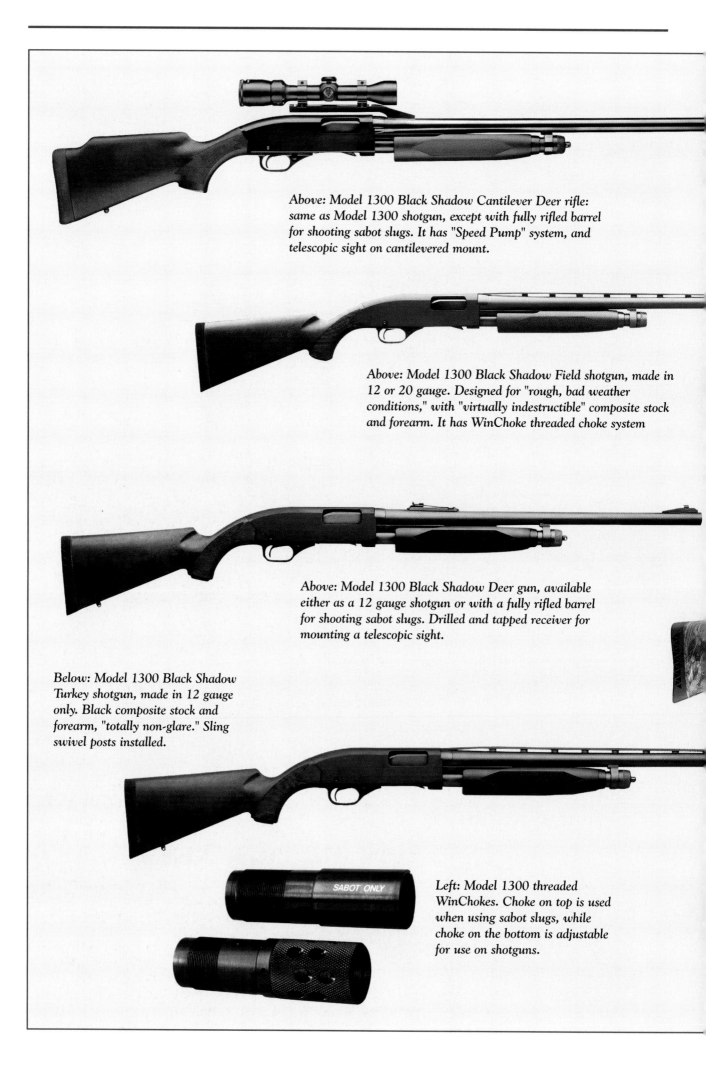

Above: Model 1300 Black Shadow Cantilever Deer rifle: same as Model 1300 shotgun, except with fully rifled barrel for shooting sabot slugs. It has "Speed Pump" system, and telescopic sight on cantilevered mount.

Above: Model 1300 Black Shadow Field shotgun, made in 12 or 20 gauge. Designed for "rough, bad weather conditions," with "virtually indestructible" composite stock and forearm. It has WinChoke threaded choke system

Above: Model 1300 Black Shadow Deer gun, available either as a 12 gauge shotgun or with a fully rifled barrel for shooting sabot slugs. Drilled and tapped receiver for mounting a telescopic sight.

Below: Model 1300 Black Shadow Turkey shotgun, made in 12 gauge only. Black composite stock and forearm, "totally non-glare." Sling swivel posts installed.

SABOT ONLY

Left: Model 1300 threaded WinChokes. Choke on top is used when using sabot slugs, while choke on the bottom is adjustable for use on shotguns.

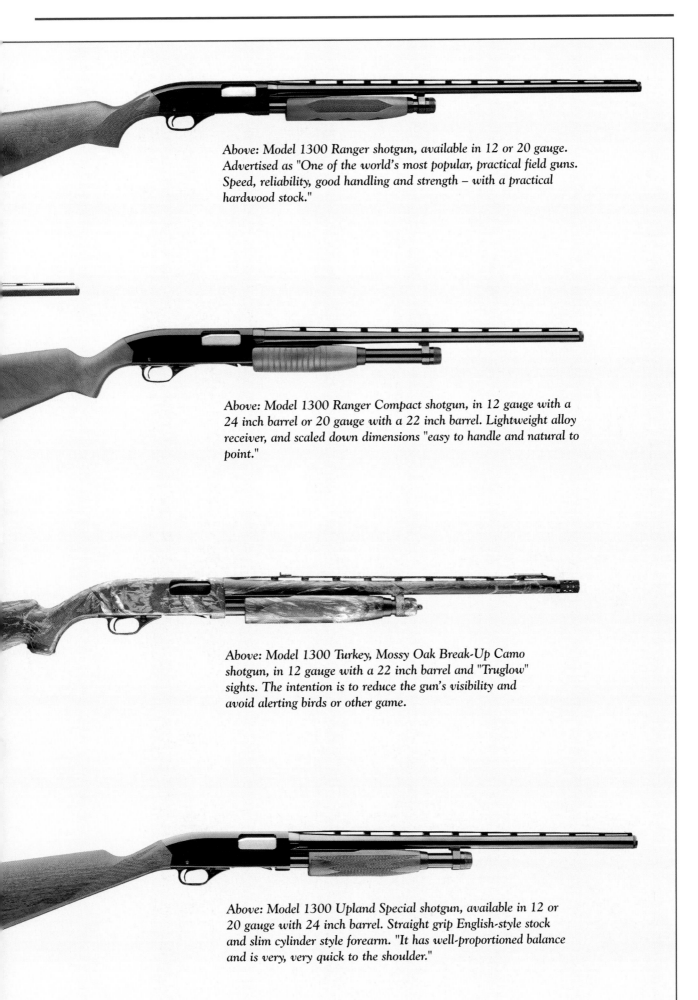

Above: Model 1300 Ranger shotgun, available in 12 or 20 gauge. Advertised as "One of the world's most popular, practical field guns. Speed, reliability, good handling and strength – with a practical hardwood stock."

Above: Model 1300 Ranger Compact shotgun, in 12 gauge with a 24 inch barrel or 20 gauge with a 22 inch barrel. Lightweight alloy receiver, and scaled down dimensions "easy to handle and natural to point."

Above: Model 1300 Turkey, Mossy Oak Break-Up Camo shotgun, in 12 gauge with a 22 inch barrel and "Truglow" sights. The intention is to reduce the gun's visibility and avoid alerting birds or other game.

Above: Model 1300 Upland Special shotgun, available in 12 or 20 gauge with 24 inch barrel. Straight grip English-style stock and slim cylinder style forearm. "It has well-proportioned balance and is very, very quick to the shoulder."

gauge, and has a 24 to 28 inch barrel. It is gas operated, with a port part way down the barrel and a piston and gas sleeve working the action, producing a softer recoil. Again several styles and sizes are offered, with features such as "Truglo" fiber optic sights for use in dim light, optional black and camouflage finish, and special types for turkey and other bird shooting.

The final shotgun model now offered is the Supreme Field and Supreme Sporting over-and-under double-barreled gun, hinged behind the receiver for folding or "breaking" to load and unload. There is a single trigger, with a selector switch to choose between the two barrels. A special feature included is a pair of strong dual locking lugs located between the barrels. An adjustable trigger and extra length barrel are provided for use in sporting clays competition.

The over-and-under model was first produced by Winchester from 1963 to 1987 at the Olin Kadensha plant in Japan. Other predecessors were single-shot and side-by-side models, now not offered. The single-shot was first produced in 1914, as a lower cost shotgun for general use. The Model 37 was then produced from 1936 to 1968, with production of over 1,000,000. The side-by-side double shotgun was the Model 21, produced from 1921 to around 1981. This was produced as an ultra high quality shotgun, competitive with those from London gunmakers such as Holland & Holland and Purdey.

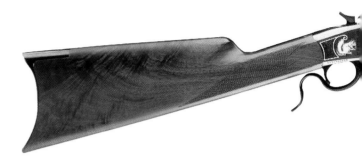

remembers from the World War II era in junior competition. This was a target-shooting rifle, and the author recollects how naturally its heavy barrel centered its peep sight on the target in prone position, providing an easy progression up the National Rifle Association scale of medals from Pro-Marksman through Sharpshooter. The Model 52 was produced up to 1980. The present Historic model is called the Model 52-B.

The other Historic rifles offered, all described in previous chapters, are the Model 1885 Low Wall .22 caliber rimfire, the Model 1886 in light weight, and the Model 1895 with caliber .405 Winchester. Engravings are also offered.

Historic rifles

These are made in Japan in Limited Edition (production held to limited quantities) and Classic Tradition (small numbers made year to year). One model in particular reflects an outstanding .22 caliber rifle, the Model 52, which the author

Custom Gun Shop

Located in the New Haven plant, the Custom Gun Shop provides extra quality versions of the Model 70 rifle, with features ordered individually by the customer. The types listed in the Year 2000 catalog are the Model 70 Custom African Express, the Model 70 Ultimate Classic, and the Model 70 Ultimate Classic Stainless.

Below: Deluxe Super-X Model 1 automatic shotgun, the predecessor to the Super-X 2 in the Year 2000 Winchester catalog. One of only 100 made in the top Pigeon Grade with engraved scene of a flight of birds.

Below: Another deluxe Super-X Model 1, engraved and with gold inlaid scene of hunting dogs and bird. Magazine capacity limited to three shells under U.S. Federal wildlife conservation laws.

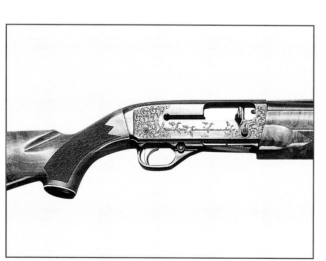
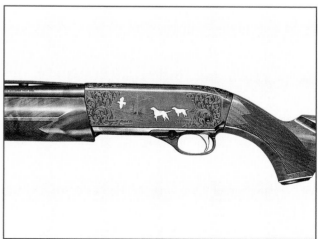

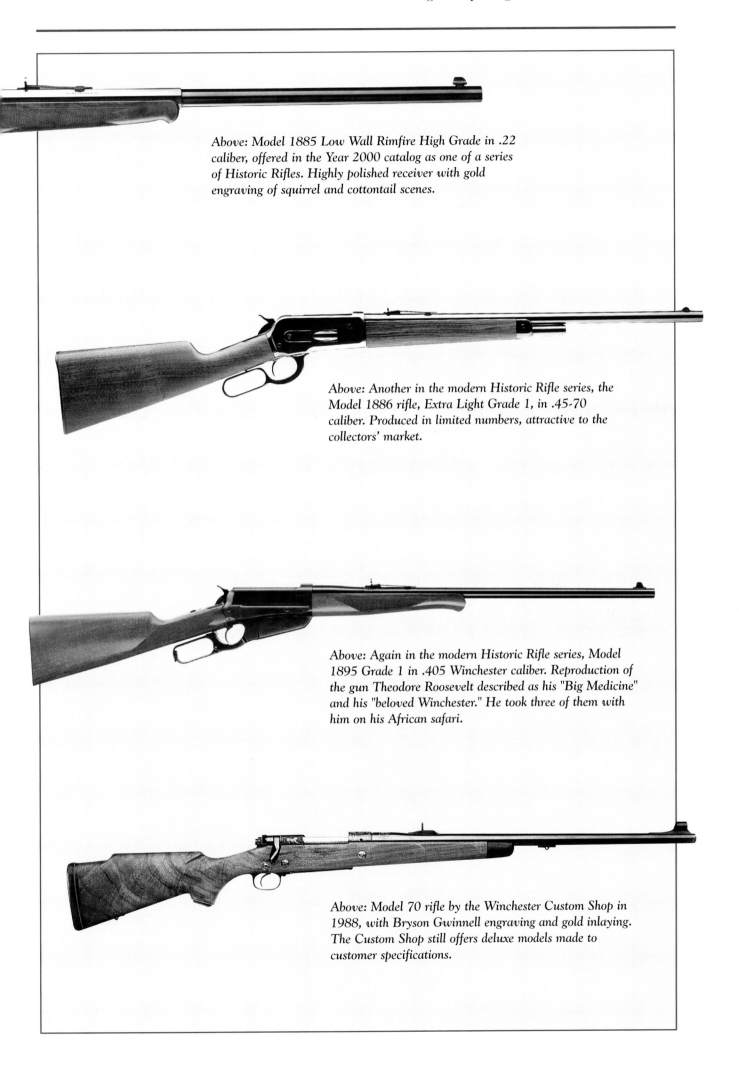

Above: Model 1885 Low Wall Rimfire High Grade in .22 caliber, offered in the Year 2000 catalog as one of a series of Historic Rifles. Highly polished receiver with gold engraving of squirrel and cottontail scenes.

Above: Another in the modern Historic Rifle series, the Model 1886 rifle, Extra Light Grade 1, in .45-70 caliber. Produced in limited numbers, attractive to the collectors' market.

Above: Again in the modern Historic Rifle series, Model 1895 Grade 1 in .405 Winchester caliber. Reproduction of the gun Theodore Roosevelt described as his "Big Medicine" and his "beloved Winchester." He took three of them with him on his African safari.

Above: Model 70 rifle by the Winchester Custom Shop in 1988, with Bryson Gwinnell engraving and gold inlaying. The Custom Shop still offers deluxe models made to customer specifications.

Future outlook;
the "gun control" controversy

R. L. Wilson, in *Winchester, An American Legend*, estimates that there are some 30 million hunters owning firearms in the United States, and some eight million who own firearms for sport shooting. Given these numbers and Winchester's fine reputation, it seems likely that the U.S. Repeating Arms Corporation and the ammunition division of the Olin Corporation will continue to flourish into the foreseeable future.

However, the present political focus on "gun control," starting with restrictions on handguns, has the potential possibility of affecting hunting and target longarms as well. Winchester's Year 2000 catalog is sensitive to this concern. Every new Winchester gun is advertised as being supplied with a gun lock, "very easy to use," preventing accidental firing, "protecting children and others." The purchaser is also referred to the National Rifle Association for information on firearms safety. It is indicated in the catalog that a portion of the sale of every Winchester firearm is donated to the Hunting and Shooting Sports Heritage Fund, formed "to help preserve and promote the rightful tradition of firearms in America."

In this writer's opinion, those are appropriate responses by Winchester to calls for "gun control." Restrictive laws tend to follow highly publicized shootings, such as in 1968 following the assassinations of Martin Luther King and Robert F. Kennedy. Arms manufacturers need to take reasonable steps toward the safe use of firearms, but at the same time need to defend themselves against unreasonable, sometimes politically motivated attacks.

Calls for the elimination of firearms in the United States are unrealistic, in view of the large number now existing, estimated at over 200 million. However, this has been attempted in other countries. Recent experiences in the United Kingdom and Australia highlight cases in point. Not only are handguns almost totally banned (must be turned in to the police) in the U.K., except for antiques, but all semiautomatic longarms

are also banned, and all other longarms except antiques must be registered. The same has happened in Australia, where laws have made even private ownership of slide action shotguns illegal. In both countries, repressive laws resulted from mass shootings by maniacs, at Dunblane, Scotland, and in Port Arthur, Australia. In both countries, the reports are that the homicide, armed robbery, and assault rates have significantly increased since the new laws went into effect.

In this writer's opinion, the U.S. Constitution may or may not prohibit gun controls,* but these should be reasonable and directly related to public safety. Gun control advocates sometimes try to make this a public health issue, but they do not carry the comparison far enough. When a new disease appears, there is a massive research effort to find a cure. The same is not true when a wave of shootings takes place. Vague movements to "Stop Gun Violence" appear, there are mothers' marches, and politicians call for new laws, their contents usually unspecified. No research is done on the actual causes of the problem or on the effectiveness of laws controlling firearms.

The benefits of the shooting sports tend to be ignored in the outcry over this issue. Federal law since 1937 has required a 10 percent excise tax on firearms and ammunition, used only for the protection of wildlife both at the Federal and State level and for the purchase of wildlife habitat, with approximately four million acres having been preserved for this purpose. Hunting is often a means of controlling excess wildlife population which damages the environment, such as with deer and geese. In regard to target shooting, this is officially recognized in the Olympic Games.

Right: Shotgun and rifle as shown in the Winchester Year 2000 catalog, each with a gun lock provided in the factory box as a safety measure. This is to prevent accidental firing, "protecting children and others."

* The Second Amendment of the Bill of Rights provides as follows: "A well regulated Militia, being necessary to the security of a free State, the right of the people to keep and bear Arms shall not be infringed."

Left: Scene of safe hunting practice, as urged by Winchester and the National Rifle Association for the millions of American hunters. The Year 2000 catalog states, "gun owners have always been extraordinarily safety conscious."

There are encouraging signs. The U.S. Centers for Disease Control and Prevention reported in November, 1999, that deaths of humans caused by guns, which started to drop two years before the Brady Law in 1981, fell 21 percent from 1993 to 1997 to the lowest level in more than 30 years, and human firearm-related injuries fell 41 percent. "Project Exile" which started in Richmond, Virginia, requiring a mandatory Federal sentence for all crimes committed with a gun, has spread to other states, and has proved effective. At the Federal level, a new program of tracing guns used in crimes has found that just 1.2 percent of Federally licensed firearms dealers sold 57 percent of the guns used in crimes, and steps are apparently under way to control these dealers.

The controversy has obvious implications for the arms collector as well as the shooter. Experience in the U.K. and Australia, and in Canada, where collectors can no longer move even antique arms freely across the international borders, shows that collecting can be seriously affected. A recent letter from a member of the Royal Armouries staff in Leeds, England, relates how he had to part with the last item in his own collection, a mint Winchester Model 1873 musket, because of the red tape involved in keeping up the required firearms certificate.

Looking to the future from a different point of view, presumably there will always be a need for military smallarms, and at this point the only American company producing them is Colt's, although the Beretta plant producing the service pistol is located in the United States, and is not American-owned. Winchester no longer has an American factory capable of ready expansion for military production as in the past. However, it may be that modern computerized machinery can quickly be adapted for such production without the large factory buildings of the past, if the Ordnance Department keeps up with the applicable technology. Experience from the support of U.S. forces in the recent Gulf War is hopeful in this regard.

Left: The Model 70 rifle has a three-position safety, allowing for locking of trigger but working of bolt. This is not found, for example, in military rifles.

COLLECTING, INVESTING, AND WHERE TO SEE THE GUNS

Winchester arms are an unusually fertile field for collecting. A tremendous variety of models, types, and calibers has been produced over a period of time extending as far back as the Civil War, each with its own gradation of rarity and value. Also, there is no sharp distinction in value between "antique," normally defined as prior to the year 1900, and "modern." Models produced as recently as the 1960s may have substantial collector's value, and for Winchester owners a cherished hunting or target gun may have become a valuable collector's item.

This chapter presents a gallery of collectible Winchester firearms, many of them rare and highly valuable, as well as some that may be seen in museums and other collections,

and some "promotional" Winchester collectibles. In some instances price guides are given, where the author is aware that the model shown has been sold at auction within the price ranges referred to. Reference to the National Rifle Association's guidelines on gun conditions would be useful if collectors are considering selling or buying firearms.

A further comment needs to be made about the effect of "gun control" laws on collecting Winchester arms. This was not a concern until recent years, except perhaps in relation to sawed-off shotguns, which have been illegal since the 1930s. In the United States there are still no Federal restrictions on buying or owning Winchester firearms except as regards purchasing through licensed dealers, but some

Left: The most deluxe grade of Model 21, and one of the rarest of all Winchesters – the Grand Royal, serial number W9190, presented to John M. Olin, with his portrait and signature on left side of frame.

Above: Half magazine .50-95 Express rifle (number 14327) with special sights and set trigger, and exquisite John Ulrich engraving, presented to Civil War General Phil Sheridan by his friend W. E. Strong.

COLLECTORS' GUN CONDITION GUIDE

The National Rifle Association standards for condition should be kept in mind by collectors, recognizing that the published price guides do not even assign values to specimens in less than "Good" condition, except for the very rarest and valuable. "Excellent" to Factory New" examples command the highest prices and have been the subjects of the largest rate of increases.

"Factory New" – all original parts; 100 percent original finish; in perfect condition in every respect, inside and out.

"Excellent" – all original parts; over 80 percent original finish; sharp lettering, numerals, and design on metal and wood; unmarred wood; fine bore.

"Fine" – all original parts; over 30 percent original finish; sharp lettering, numerals, and design on metal and wood; minor marks in wood; fine bore.

"Very Good" – all original parts; none to 30 percent original finish; original metal surfaces smooth with all edges sharp; clear lettering, numerals, and design on metal; wood slightly scratched or bruised; bore disregarded for collectors' firearms.

"Good" – some minor replacement parts; metal smoothly rusted or lightly pitted in places, cleaned or reblued; principal lettering, numerals, and design on metal legible; wood refinished, scratched, bruised or minor cracks repaired; in good working order.

"Fair" – some major parts replaced; minor replacement parts may be required; metal rusted, may be lightly pitted all over, vigorously cleaned or reblued; rounded edges of metal and wood; principal lettering, numerals, and design on metal partly obliterated; wood scratched, bruised, cracked or repaired where broken; in fair working order or can be easily repaired and placed in working order.

"Poor" – major and minor parts replaced; replacement parts required and extensive restoration needed; metal deeply pitted; principal lettering, numerals, and design obliterated; wood badly scratched, bruised, cracked or broken; mechanically inoperative; generally undesirable as a collector's item.

states have their own restrictions. In New Jersey, for example, an M1 carbine, some of which were made by Winchester, is considered an "assault rifle" and it is illegal to have one (the excuse for this is that it can take a magazine with more than eight shots), and in order to purchase any kind of firearm or ammunition it is necessary to have a Firearms Purchase Permit issued through the local Police Department, together with a background check and fingerprinting. Hopefully in the future, antique firearms – those models made before 1900 and for which ammunition is not commercially available – will be exempted from most controls, but this is not assured.

Together with Colt's, Winchesters have been the "blue chip" of gun collecting for increases in value since the hobby began a spectacular rise in the 1950s. For example, the 1999 Second Edition of the R .L. Wilson *Price Guide to Gun Collecting* values a Henry rifle in "excellent" condition at $50,000, and a 1 of 1,000 Model 1873 at $125,000. Winchesters that can be shown to have been owned by famous personages or engraved examples presented to them can be valued for much more. The author's collection is not in this range, but he tells his wife, upon acquiring another gun, that this is not actually spending money, it's investing!

Additional price guides include, for arms made before 1900, *Flayderman's Guide to Antique American Firearms*, and – for more recent models – S.P. Fjestad's *Blue Book of Gun Values*. Readers following the successive editions of these books over the past 15 to 20 years will note that the

Above: The U.S. Constitution 200th Anniversary Model 94, one of only eight built exclusively for Cherry's of Greensboro, N. Carolina, the leading commemorative dealer. Engraving is by Bottega C. Giovanelli.

percentage increase in values has been substantially more for Winchesters and Colts than for most other makes. The general rate of increase in the arms collecting field has been 10 percent a year, and it is notable that, unlike the financial markets, values have not decreased in any one year, although there has been some fluctuation in the rate of increase. As in other fields of collecting, condition is a prime determinant.

Among Winchester and related firearms from before 1900 the Henry rifle is the overall star, valued in a range up to around $40,000 today. Engraved and presentation models may fetch more, although there have been rumors of engraving having been added to some

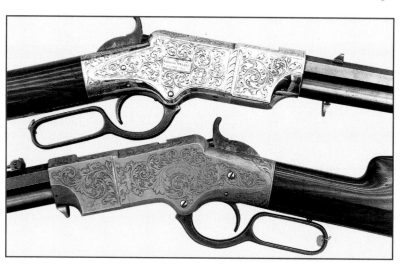

Left: Important Civil War period presentation Henry Rifles: top, serial number 9, presented to Gideon Welles, Secretary of the Navy, and bottom, serial number 1, to Edwin M. Stanton, Secretary of War. Oliver Winchester made relatively few such "promotional" presentations, as compared to his contemporary, Samuel Colt.

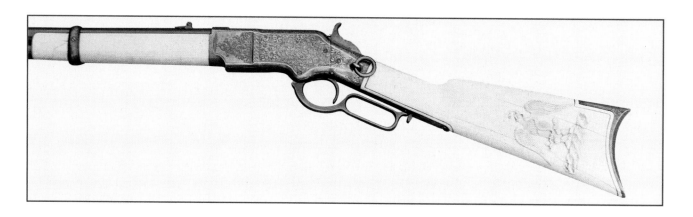

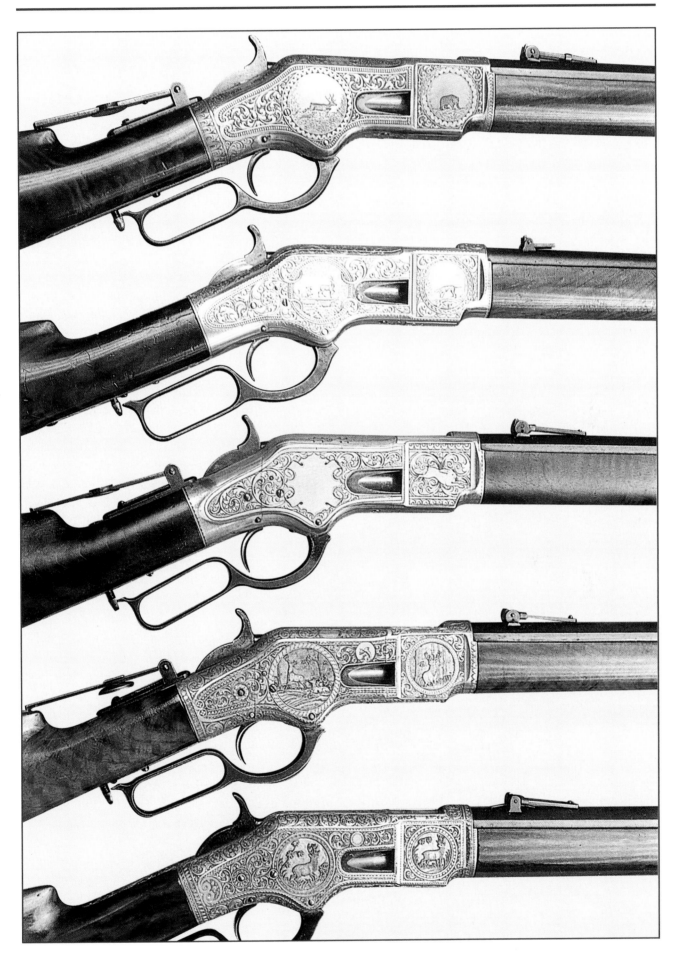

Left: Ivory-stocked Model 1866, number 21921, from the private collection of Mexican President Porfirio Diaz, boasting Mexican eagle on its stock.

Above: Deluxe Model 1866 rifles, with engraving attributed to John and Conrad Ulrich (and possibly one by Herman – no signed rifles by him have been found).

specimens in modern times (the writer has seen no reports of entire arms being faked). Somewhat strangely, the earlier and more scarce Volcanic rifles and pistols have lower valuations, in the $10,000 range, perhaps pointing to a collecting opportunity.

The Model 1866 Winchester, the "Yellow Boy," is very much in demand, with values in the $5,000 range and up. Rifle and carbine variations are generally comparable in value, as are those with round or octagonal barrels, but the scarcer musket variations command premium prices, a pattern continuing through the Model 1892.

The Model 1873, made in much larger quantities, is widely available to collectors. The black powder model up to about 1890 is the most desirable. The "1 of 100" and "1 of 1000" variations as discussed in earlier chapters have values up to the $100,000 range, but collectors should beware, since these firearms are susceptible to faking, since only the marking distinguishes these from other highly finished rifles. Regular

Model 1873s in fine condition are $1,000 to $2,000 in value.

Prices increase for the large, impressive Model 1876 and Model 1886, to the $5,000 to $10,000 range. The Model 1892 and Model 1894 are more widely available, in the $1,000 to $2,000 range for lower (meaning earlier) serial numbers; there are published tables correlating serial numbers to the year of manufacture. Prices for Model 1895 military type and single-shot rifles and also shotguns increase again, to $2,000 and upwards.

Among Winchesters produced since 1900, the pre-1964 Model 70 hunting rifle is particularly prized and has increased in value, because of the change in the manufacturing process and the real or supposed reduction in quality which took place at that time. An article in the 1999 *Blue Book*, "Buying Tomorrow's Collectibles Today," recommends watching the values assigned to earlier Winchesters and buying them when the price of new guns approaches this level, based on the theory that the old guns will subsequently increase in more in value.

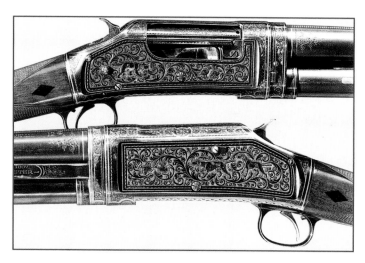

Another field of collecting modern guns is in commemorative issues. Winchester itself went into this field in 1964 when the company was approached by the Wyoming Diamond Jubilee Committee, and produced 1,500 Model 94 carbines engraved with lettering and pictures in honor of this anniversary. Sales went so well that the company produced some 50 more commemorative models up to 1986. In that year, the company made over 112,000 of a Buffalo Bill commemorative, which some collectors felt tended to spoil the market since a part of the appeal of commemoratives is that they are normally issued in limited numbers.

The Wyoming Diamond Jubilee Model was sold in 1964 for $100 but in 1999 had a value of $1,295, according to the *Blue Book*. In any event, America Remembers, a company in Virginia, currently offers a line of some 25 commemorative Winchesters in editions limited to 300 each, by makers such as Uberti

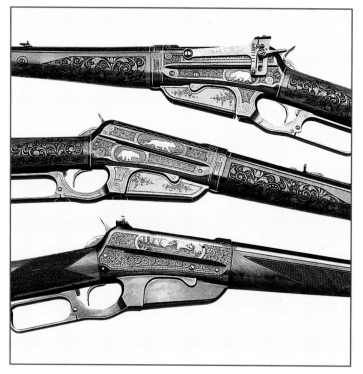

Above left: Exquisite matched pair of Model 1897 rifles, serial numbers 1 and 2, engraved and signed by John Ulrich, with dogs and game birds within scrollwork instead of set in panels.

Left: Superbly engraved Model 1895 rifles. Top, serial number 88044, with J.U. signature of John Ulrich on lower tang, chambered for .30-06 cartridge, and owned by author Zane Grey. Center, takedown rifle in .405 caliber, serial number 78191, signed by John Ulrich. Bottom, also a .405 caliber rifle, serial number, probably engraved by Angelo Stokes, active with Winchester from 1905 to 1917.

Right: Model 1873 in .22 rimfire, beautifully crafted with factory engraving and cheekpiece pistol-grip stock and shotgun buttplate.

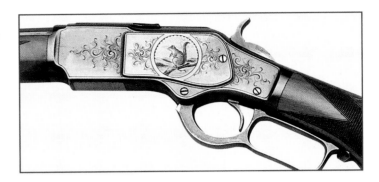

Below right: Commemorative musket and rifle which were among the arms issued to celebrate the National Rifle Association's Centennial in 1971, recognizing the NRA's contribution to marksmanship, safety, and firearms education.

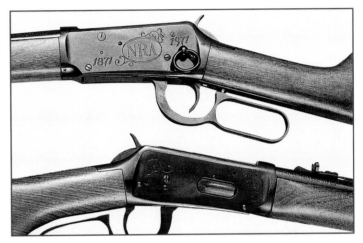

of Italy, and these presumably will increase in value in the future.

Winchesters are particularly accessible to collectors because most local gun shops will have used Winchester arms available as well as the new models, which are widely distributed. Shops specializing in antique arms usually feature Winchesters, but the number of such shops has been decreasing.

Most dealers and individual collectors now display their items for sale at gun shows, which are held in many locations around the United States on a periodic basis of two or more a year. These are divided into two kinds: those allowing only antiques, generally those made before 1900; and commercial gun shows, sometimes of a flea market type, which include modern guns and also gun-related items. For better or worse, the commercial gun shows in particular have recently come under fire by the "gun control" movement. Laws have been proposed to require a waiting period of more than two days for background checks of purchasers, which would put the shows out of business, since these are usually held only on weekends. Presumably shows with only antiques would not be affected, but such shows already tend not to be held in states with special restrictions, such as New Jersey.

In any event, shows specializing in antiques still have large attendances and substantial numbers of high quality arms for sale. Two of the periodicals listed in the bibliography carry schedules of such shows. An admission charge of only $5 to $10 per day is charged,

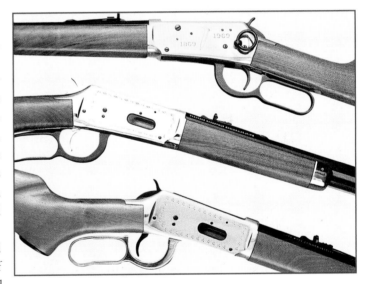

Above right: Winchester commemoratives: top, Centennial of the East-West rail connection (Golden Spike, Promontory Point, Utah, 1869); center, the life of sportsman-conservationist Theodore Roosevelt; bottom, the 125th anniversary of the state of Texas.

Right: Fabulous single-shot Winchesters engraved and signed by John Ulrich: top, number 96428 (with two signatures); and bottom, number 110806, a takedown which was issued with two No. 3 barrels.

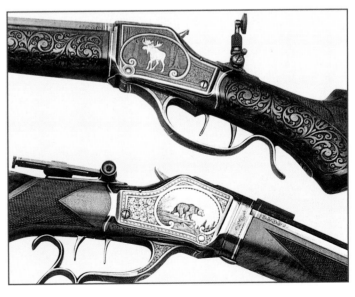

Above: Winchester display at the Year 2000 "Shot Show" in Las Vegas, the trade show for manufacturers and dealers. This was held concurrently with the Las Vegas Gun Show, one of the premier antique guns shows for collectors, open to the public, unlike the "Shot Show."

and there are often educational displays as well as sales tables sometimes numbering in the hundreds. The tables are rented by collectors as well as professional dealers, and persons with individual items to sell are welcome to bring these in. Winchesters are among the most popular items, and it is noteworthy that prices tend to follow those in the published guides, particularly *Flayderman's*.

An increasingly important development in recent years has been auctions of collectors' arms and armor, held by an increasing number of companies, including famous names like Sotheby's, Christie's, and Butterfield and Butterfield. There is sometimes the impression at gun shows that fine quality items are disappearing from the market, but recent auction catalogs seem to suggest that large collections formed in earlier years are now coming up for sale at auctions. This seems to be particularly true of top condition and engraved and presentation

Left: One of the strangest sites where enthusiasts can view Winchester firearms and other collectibles is the Winchester Mystery House, designated a California Registered Historical Landmark, in San Jose. There are many other fine collections of Winchester firearms at museums across the United States.

Winchesters. Whether this will continue, and whether present purchases will turn out to be bargains in the future, is an open question. It may be significant that Butterfield and Butterfield has been purchased by Ebay, which conducts Internet auctions, but such auctions for firearms may have legal problems, and also many collectors want to see and handle guns before they make bids.

There are many local collectors' clubs, and also a national organization, the Winchester Arms Collectors' Association, which are valuable and enjoyable for aspiring collectors. The number on the author's membership card for the Winchester Arms Collector's Association is 4,951, indicating a substantial membership. It publishes a quarterly magazine and holds an annual meeting and gun show in Cody, Wyoming, the site of the Buffalo Bill Historical Center, which has the world's largest collection of Winchester arms. The Association also co-sponsors other shows such as in Springfield, Massachusetts, and Reno, Nevada. The magazines listed in the bibliography also carry articles about Winchester arms, notably *American Rifleman*, which is published by the National Rifle Association for its membership of some 3,000,000.

Fine collections of Winchester arms can be seen at a number of arms and armor museums around the United States, which in too many cases are not well known to the general public. The largest collection, as mentioned above, is at the Buffalo Bill Historical Center in Cody, Wyoming, an historic community established by the famous Indian scout

and showman himself, at the entrance to Yellowstone National Park. The Center's Cody Firearms Museum covers the entire history of firearms, but in particular includes some 3,500 Winchester arms with the original Winchester company collection started by Oliver Winchester.

Probably next in scope and importance is the Winchester collection at the Gene Autry Museum of Western Heritage located in Griffith Park in Los Angeles, California. However, this may be equaled or exceeded by the National Firearms Museum of the National Rifle Association in Fairfax, Virginia. Some of the rarest and most historic Winchesters are at the Smithsonian Institution in Washington, D.C., although arms displays have unfortunately been de-emphasized there in recent years. Other notable Winchester collections are at the Woolaroc Museum in Bartlesville, Oklahoma, and at the National Cowboy Hall of Fame Museum in Oklahoma City. The U.S. Military Academy at West Point, near New York City, has a fine and recently expanded museum showing Winchester's American military arms.

For arms collectors, including the author, an attraction of Winchesters is that they are not just outdated historic artifacts, but are still eminently practical, as well as esthetically pleasing.

Below: Aside from firearms, there is much memorabilia for Winchester enthusiasts to collect, some, like these from the Winchester-Olin and U.S. Repeating Arms periods, mainly promotional items not produced by the factory.

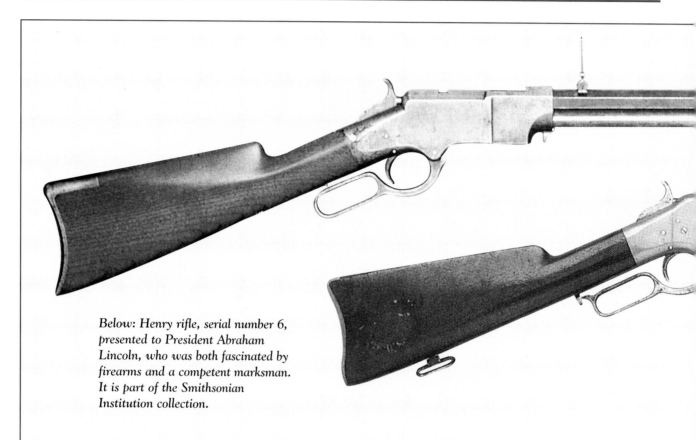

Below: Henry rifle, serial number 6, presented to President Abraham Lincoln, who was both fascinated by firearms and a competent marksman. It is part of the Smithsonian Institution collection.

Above: Model 1866 saddle ring carbine, serial number 45903, in .44 caliber, with 20in barrel with standard sights and full magazine; factory engraved, its frame features a bullfight scene on left and initial "NE" on right. Value, approx $8,000 to $12,000.

Left: Rare presentation Henry Model 1860 rifle, serial number 1, one of the most historic and important American antique firearms, presented to Edwin M. Stanton, who was Lincoln's Secretary of War.

Above: Scarce Model 1866 lever action military musket, serial number 50800, in .44 caliber with 27in blued barrel, standard sights, three bands, and walnut stock. Value, approx $5,000.

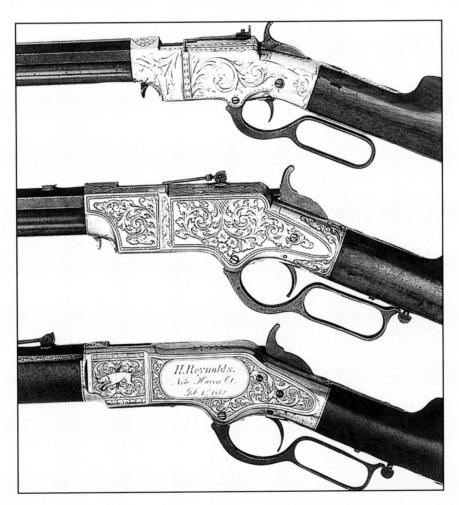

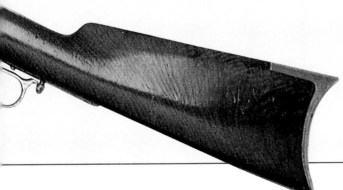

Above: Firearms such as these are collectors' favorites: top, the Volcanic; center, the Henry; and bottom a rifle presented to H. Reynolds (a supplier of parts to Winchester) in 1872. The brass frames are finished an silver and gold plating.

Above: Rare Model 1873 One of One Hundred, serial number 27179, .44 caliber, with 26in octagonal barrel, mid-range Vernier tang sight, and deluxe checkered straight stock and fore-end. (See detail.)

Right: Model 1873 lever action musket, serial number 50597B, in .44 W.C.F. caliber, with 30in round barrel, blued finish, and oil-finished fore-end and buttstock. Value: $5,000-7,000.

Below: Rare factory engraved Third Model 1873 Short rifle, serial number 549178B, in .44-40 caliber, with 20in octagonal barrel with full set magazine, folding three-leaf sight, and set trigger. Value: $30,000-40,000.

Below: Model 1873, serial number 654955, in .38 W.C.F. caliber – a Third Model with rare 22in octagonal barrel with full magazine, Sheard foresight, tang-mounted peep sight, deluxe walnut fore-end and pistol-grip stock. Value: $20,000-30,000.

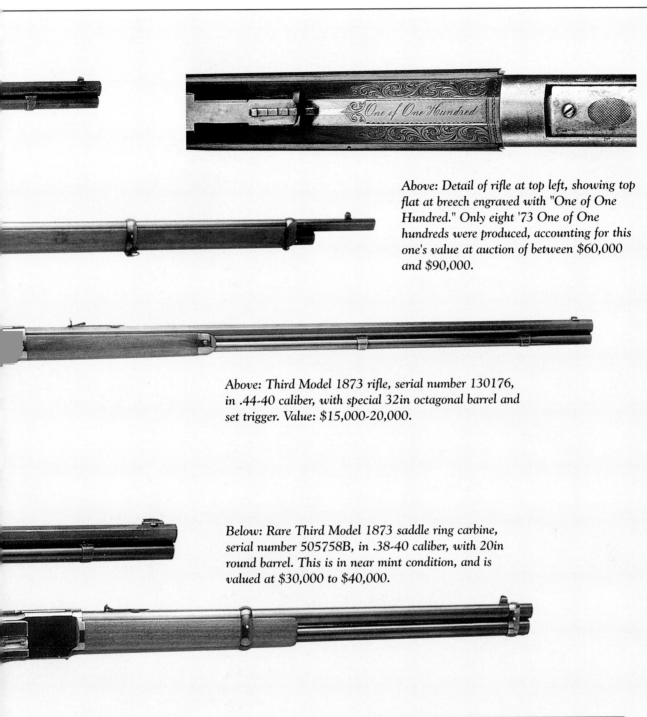

Above: Detail of rifle at top left, showing top flat at breech engraved with "One of One Hundred." Only eight '73 One of One hundreds were produced, accounting for this one's value at auction of between $60,000 and $90,000.

Above: Third Model 1873 rifle, serial number 130176, in .44-40 caliber, with special 32in octagonal barrel and set trigger. Value: $15,000-20,000.

Below: Rare Third Model 1873 saddle ring carbine, serial number 505758B, in .38-40 caliber, with 20in round barrel. This is in near mint condition, and is valued at $30,000 to $40,000.

ht: One of six Model 1873s in the gun n at Sandringham, the home of Her esty Queen Elizabeth II and the Duke dinburgh. Apparently, these arms are nants of presentations by Edward, ce of Wales, while traveling through ia in 1875

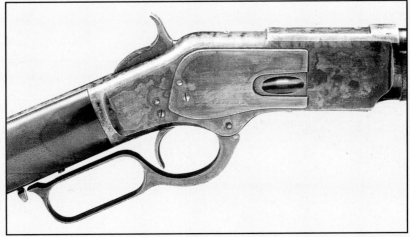

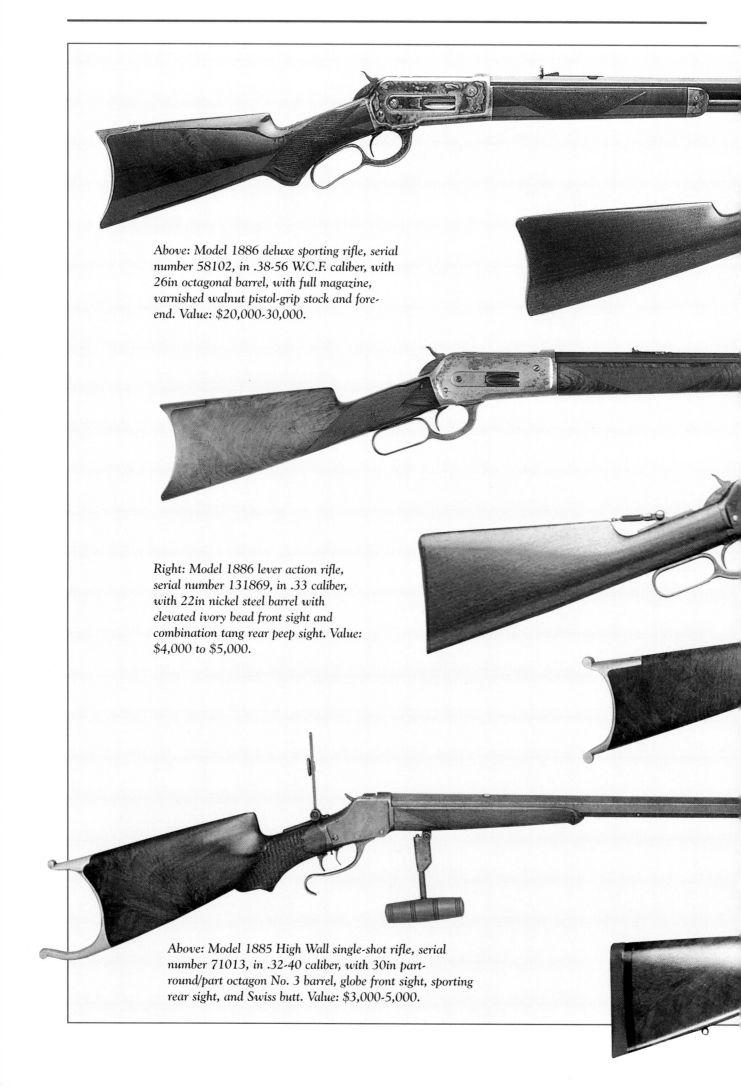

Above: Model 1886 deluxe sporting rifle, serial number 58102, in .38-56 W.C.F. caliber, with 26in octagonal barrel, with full magazine, varnished walnut pistol-grip stock and fore-end. Value: $20,000-30,000.

Right: Model 1886 lever action rifle, serial number 131869, in .33 caliber, with 22in nickel steel barrel with elevated ivory bead front sight and combination tang rear peep sight. Value: $4,000 to $5,000.

Above: Model 1885 High Wall single-shot rifle, serial number 71013, in .32-40 caliber, with 30in part-round/part octagon No. 3 barrel, globe front sight, sporting rear sight, and Swiss butt. Value: $3,000-5,000.

Above: Rare Model 1886 saddle ring carbine, serial number 59173, in .45-70 caliber, with 22in round barrel blued and casehardened, standard walnut stock and carbine-style butt. Value: $30,000-40,000.

Left: Another Model 1886 rifle, in plain finish with no extra decoration, half magazine with tang peep sight. The half magazine is for lighter weight for hunting.

Above: Model 1885 High Wall single-shot rifle, serial number 66337, in .32-40 caliber, with octagonal barrel with Globe front sight and mid-range tang sight, double set triggers, and Helm butt. Value: $2,000-3,000.

Below: Model 1886 rifle, serial number 145592, a takedown in .33 W.C.F. caliber, beautifully engraved by Angelo J. Stokes. English proofmarks suggest sale or display there; some Winchesters were sold through London gunmakers Holland & Holland and Boss & Co.

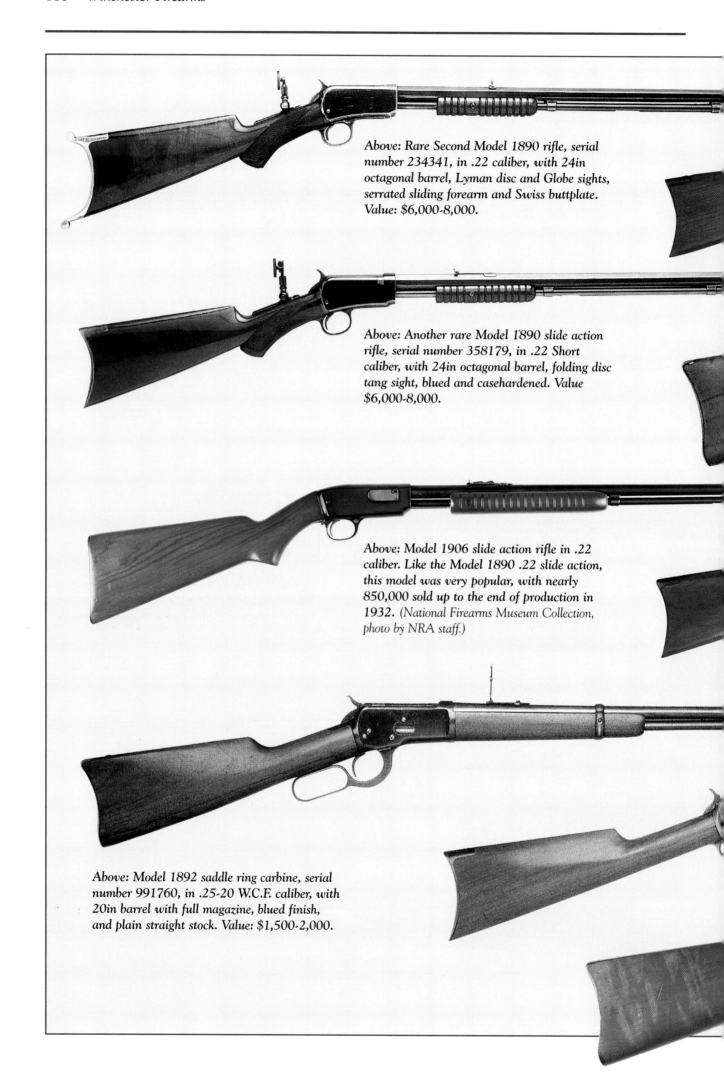

Above: Rare Second Model 1890 rifle, serial number 234341, in .22 caliber, with 24in octagonal barrel, Lyman disc and Globe sights, serrated sliding forearm and Swiss buttplate. Value: $6,000-8,000.

Above: Another rare Model 1890 slide action rifle, serial number 358179, in .22 Short caliber, with 24in octagonal barrel, folding disc tang sight, blued and casehardened. Value $6,000-8,000.

Above: Model 1906 slide action rifle in .22 caliber. Like the Model 1890 .22 slide action, this model was very popular, with nearly 850,000 sold up to the end of production in 1932. *(National Firearms Museum Collection, photo by NRA staff.)*

Above: Model 1892 saddle ring carbine, serial number 991760, in .25-20 W.C.F. caliber, with 20in barrel with full magazine, blued finish, and plain straight stock. Value: $1,500-2,000.

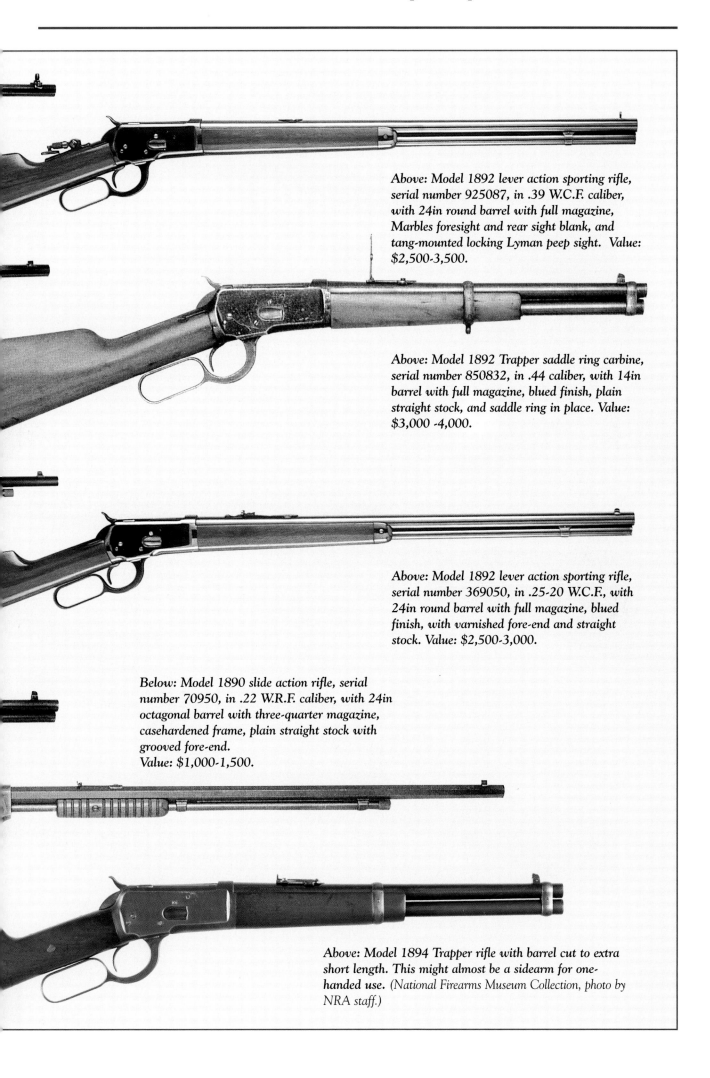

Above: Model 1892 lever action sporting rifle, serial number 925087, in .39 W.C.F. caliber, with 24in round barrel with full magazine, Marbles foresight and rear sight blank, and tang-mounted locking Lyman peep sight. Value: $2,500-3,500.

Above: Model 1892 Trapper saddle ring carbine, serial number 850832, in .44 caliber, with 14in barrel with full magazine, blued finish, plain straight stock, and saddle ring in place. Value: $3,000 -4,000.

Above: Model 1892 lever action sporting rifle, serial number 369050, in .25-20 W.C.F., with 24in round barrel with full magazine, blued finish, with varnished fore-end and straight stock. Value: $2,500-3,000.

Below: Model 1890 slide action rifle, serial number 70950, in .22 W.R.F. caliber, with 24in octagonal barrel with three-quarter magazine, casehardened frame, plain straight stock with grooved fore-end.
Value: $1,000-1,500.

Above: Model 1894 Trapper rifle with barrel cut to extra short length. This might almost be a sidearm for one-handed use. (National Firearms Museum Collection, photo by NRA staff.)

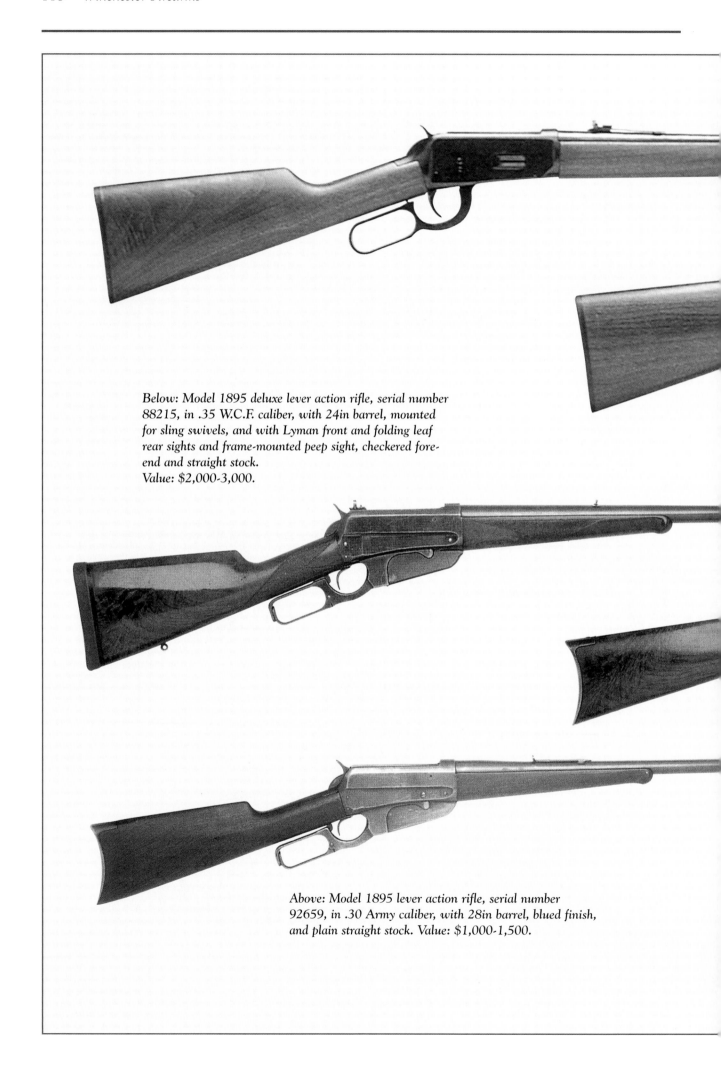

Below: Model 1895 deluxe lever action rifle, serial number 88215, in .35 W.C.F. caliber, with 24in barrel, mounted for sling swivels, and with Lyman front and folding leaf rear sights and frame-mounted peep sight, checkered fore-end and straight stock.
Value: $2,000-3,000.

Above: Model 1895 lever action rifle, serial number 92659, in .30 Army caliber, with 28in barrel, blued finish, and plain straight stock. Value: $1,000-1,500.

Left: Model 1894 Trapper saddle ring carbine, serial number 5010443, in .30-30 caliber, with 16in barrel with standard sights, blued finish, satin finished walnut stock with shotgun-style butt. Value: $700-900.

Above: Model 1894 Trapper carbine, serial number 4981243, in .30-30 caliber, with 16in barrel, blued finish. Contained in the original factory carton, this specimen was valued at auction at $800-1,200.

Below: Model 1895 deluxe lever action rifle, serial number 6980, in .30 U.S. caliber, with 26in barrel with rear sight blank and frame-mounted Lyman peep sight, blued finish, checkered wrist and straight stock. Value: $1,500-2,000.

Below: A rare offering at auction indeed! An extraordinary crate of ten Model 1895 saddle ring carbines in .30 Army caliber, each with 21.5in barrel, blued finish, oil-finished walnut stock and fore-end, and retaining original yellow hang tag. All the carbines unfired. Value: $60,000-80,000.

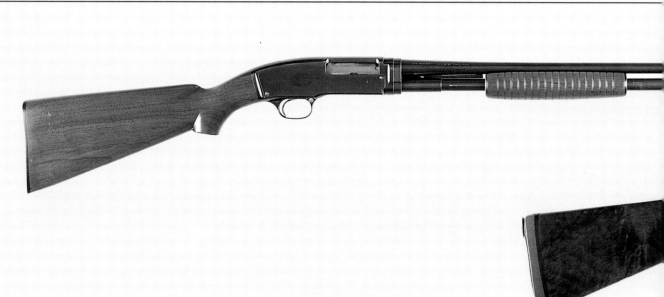

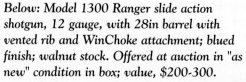

Below: Model 1300 Ranger slide action shotgun, 12 gauge, with 28in barrel with vented rib and WinChoke attachment; blued finish; walnut stock. Offered at auction in "as new" condition in box; value, $200-300.

Below: Riot and trench guns with police and military applications. Top, Model 1893 riot gun, 12 gauge. Center, Model 1897 riot gun, issued to Illinois State Police. Bottom, Model 1897 trench gun, with carrying sling and bayonet, plus packet of 25 military-issue shotshells; ventilated hand guard over barrel assisted in cooling when barrels heated up after repeated firing.

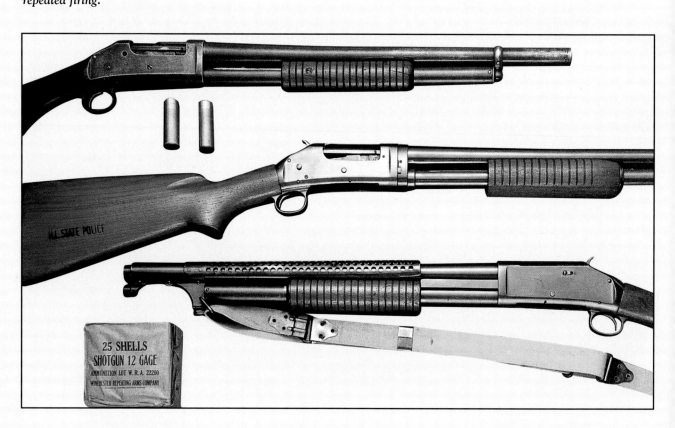

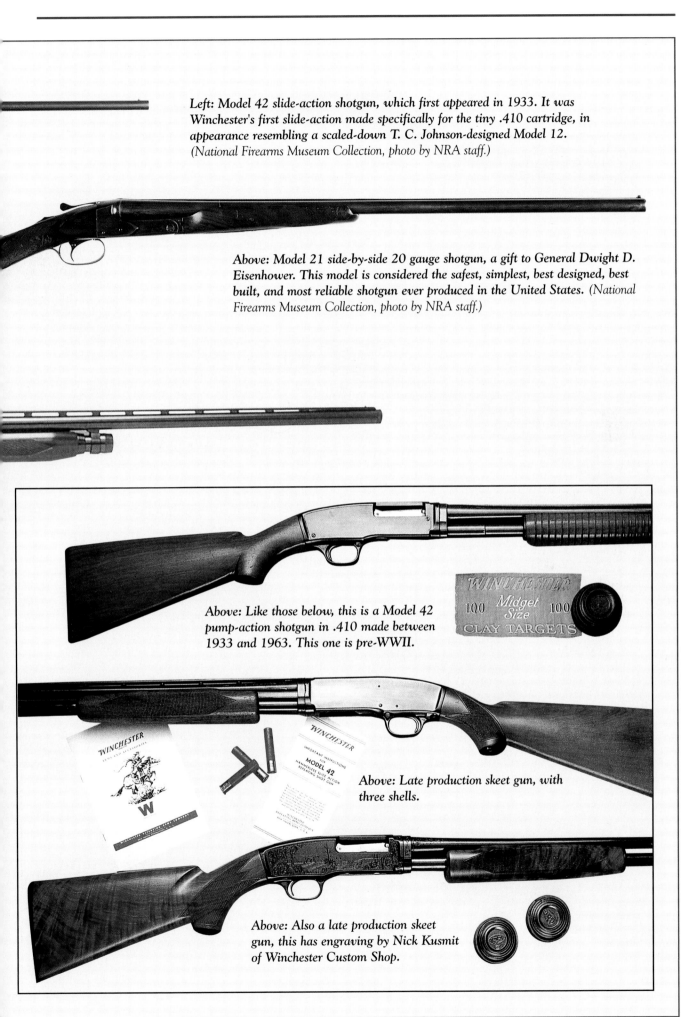

Left: *Model 42 slide-action shotgun, which first appeared in 1933. It was Winchester's first slide-action made specifically for the tiny .410 cartridge, in appearance resembling a scaled-down T. C. Johnson-designed Model 12. (National Firearms Museum Collection, photo by NRA staff.)*

Above: *Model 21 side-by-side 20 gauge shotgun, a gift to General Dwight D. Eisenhower. This model is considered the safest, simplest, best designed, best built, and most reliable shotgun ever produced in the United States. (National Firearms Museum Collection, photo by NRA staff.)*

Above: *Like those below, this is a Model 42 pump-action shotgun in .410 made between 1933 and 1963. This one is pre-WWII.*

Above: *Late production skeet gun, with three shells.*

Above: *Also a late production skeet gun, this has engraving by Nick Kusmit of Winchester Custom Shop.*

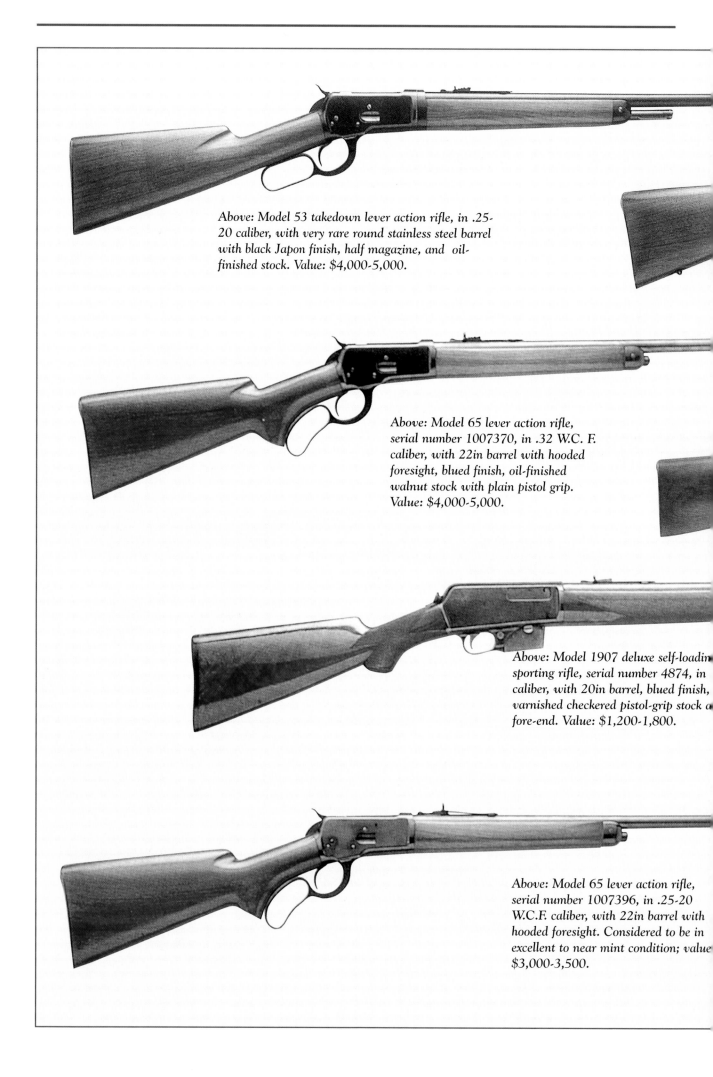

Above: Model 53 takedown lever action rifle, in .25-20 caliber, with very rare round stainless steel barrel with black Japon finish, half magazine, and oil-finished stock. Value: $4,000-5,000.

Above: Model 65 lever action rifle, serial number 1007370, in .32 W.C. F. caliber, with 22in barrel with hooded foresight, blued finish, oil-finished walnut stock with plain pistol grip. Value: $4,000-5,000.

Above: Model 1907 deluxe self-loading sporting rifle, serial number 4874, in caliber, with 20in barrel, blued finish, varnished checkered pistol-grip stock a fore-end. Value: $1,200-1,800.

Above: Model 65 lever action rifle, serial number 1007396, in .25-20 W.C.F. caliber, with 22in barrel with hooded foresight. Considered to be in excellent to near mint condition; value $3,000-3,500.

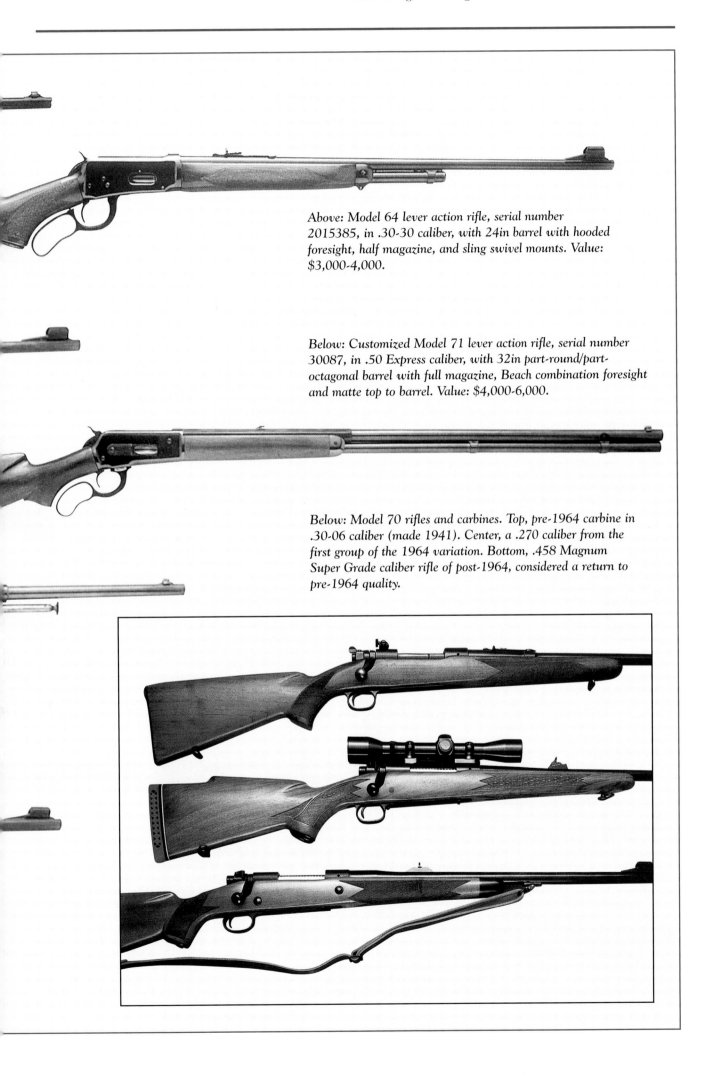

Above: Model 64 lever action rifle, serial number 2015385, in .30-30 caliber, with 24in barrel with hooded foresight, half magazine, and sling swivel mounts. Value: $3,000-4,000.

Below: Customized Model 71 lever action rifle, serial number 30087, in .50 Express caliber, with 32in part-round/part-octagonal barrel with full magazine, Beach combination foresight and matte top to barrel. Value: $4,000-6,000.

Below: Model 70 rifles and carbines. Top, pre-1964 carbine in .30-06 caliber (made 1941). Center, a .270 caliber from the first group of the 1964 variation. Bottom, .458 Magnum Super Grade caliber rifle of post-1964, considered a return to pre-1964 quality.

FIRING THE GUNS

The accompanying tabulation shows a comparison of the power and accuracy of a selection of Winchester arms from the Henry rifle through the World War II M1 Garand and M1 Carbine. The results are partly from test firing on a range near the author's home in New Jersey, using a chronometer to measure muzzle velocity. All the arms used were original, and were in good to fine condition. Assistance was provided by Angus Laidlaw, a contributing editor of *American Rifleman* magazine.

Although informal rather than rigorous, the test gave a "hands on" feel and confirmation of what might be expected from the different purposes of the arms involved. It may be noted that no mechanical problems were found even though the guns fired are over 100 years old (the Model 1873 rifle was made in 1884, from its serial number). All worked as originally designed!

Some conclusions from this test are as follows:

The Henry rifle has been criticized as using a low power pistol-type cartridge. However, its muzzle velocity compares with the later Winchester Model 1873 and Model 1892 hunting rifles, which are still used effectively for game up to the size of deer. Certainly the Henry was less powerful than the Model 1861 Springfield type rifle musket which was the main infantry weapon of the Civil War; a similar firing test by the author for his companion volume, *Colt Firearms*, showed a muzzle velocity for that model of 972 foot pounds. In contrast, the .44 caliber 1860 Colt Army pistol showed a muzzle velocity of only 336 foot pounds, and the Model 1911 Automatic of only 328. The Henry was more powerful than a pistol, and in the author's opinion, it was not that much less

powerful than the 1861 rifle musket to justify the Army not adopting it for extensive use.

The Model 1883 Hotchkiss with its large .45-70 cartridge was effective for military use, and with its seven-shot capacity should have been adopted by the Army instead of having the Springfield Armory make over 200,000 of the Model 1884 single-shot trapdoor rifles.

The M1 Garand rifle shows high power and accuracy, as would be expected. Conversely, however, the M1 Carbine shows limited power. Still, considering that the carbine was intended as a replacement for the Model 1911 semiautomatic pistol, which the author's test showed to have less than half the carbine's muzzle energy, and in view of its use by and popularity with the troops using it, this does not seem unreasonable.

The relative lack of precision target grouping shown for the Model 1873 and Hotchkiss rifles reflects the black powder cartridges used, as well as perhaps the used condition of the guns, and the shooter's lack of expertise. The better results from the Model 1892 are probably because of the modern smokeless powder cartridge and the better design of the rifle. All these rifles were comfortable to shoot, without excessive recoil or tendency to pull to the side.

Although test results are not directly shown for the M1 Garand and the M1 Carbine, the author has fired both these rifles on previous occasions. He qualified with the carbine while serving in the National Guard in earlier days, and has fired his National Match Garand* on

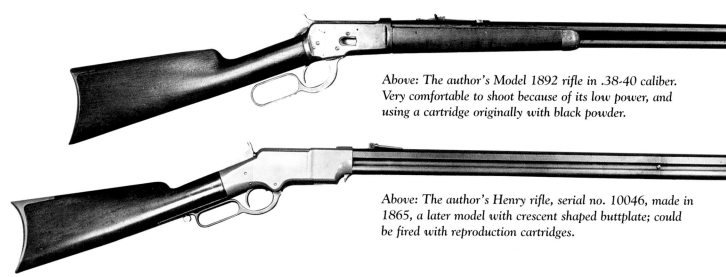

Above: The author's Model 1892 rifle in .38-40 caliber. Very comfortable to shoot because of its low power, and using a cartridge originally with black powder.

Above: The author's Henry rifle, serial no. 10046, made in 1865, a later model with crescent shaped buttplate; could be fired with reproduction cartridges.

The Springfield Armory pulled out rifles testing as particularly accurate for issue to participants in the annual Camp Perry, Ohio, matches. The author was fortunate to receive one of these in a sale of surplus rifles through the DCM in the 1960s.

Right: The author firing his Model 1892 rifle, at his local rifle club with outdoor range but enclosed shed for noise suppression. Ear protection temporarily omitted!

repeated occasions in Director of Civilian Marksmanship (DCM) reported matches at his local gun club (the DCM office provides ammunition for clubs reporting members participating on 60-round matches). The Garand is accurate and reliable! – although its power is brought forcefully home to the shooter through its noise and recoil. The carbine is more comfortable to shoot, and still has a surprising feel of power, and accuracy at a 200-yard range. It should be noted that the writer owns an M1 Carbine, now not kept in his home state of New Jersey, with only the 8-round clip that came with the rifle when purchased from the government through the DCM; it seems unreasonable for the State of New Jersey to consider and outlaw this as an "assault rifle," for owners not possessing larger-capacity clips.

Above: The author firing his Model 1883 Hotchkiss carbine; ear protection used. The heavy .45-70 cartridge causes the rifle's muzzle to rise, but the "kick" was not found excessive.

Model	Powder charge, grains of black powder	Bullet weight, grains	Muzzle velocity, feet per second	Muzzle energy, foot pounds	Hand rest three-shot target group (in inches at 75 feet
1860 Henry rifle, .44 caliber	28	200	1,150	594	*
Model 1873 rifle, .44-40 caliber	40	205	1,306	776	6
Model 1883 Hotchkiss carbine, .45-70 caliber	70	405	1,360	1663	6
Model 1892, .38-40 caliber	40	173	1,005	390	4
M1 Garand .30-06 caliber	**	150	2,740	2500	2
M1 Carbine, .30 caliber	**	110	1,900	882	*

* Firing test not done: no cartridges available for Henry; M1 Carbine illegal in New Jersey. Data from *Cartridges of the World* (see bibliography).

** Not applicable; smokeless powder, standard government cartridges.

BIBLIOGRAPHY

BOOKS

Barnes, Frank C., *Cartridges of the World* (Iola, WI, DBI Books, 1998).

Blackmore, Howard L., *Guns and Rifles of the World* (New York, NY: Viking Press, 1965).

Browning, John, and Gentry, Curt, *John M. Browning, American Gun Maker* (Garden City, NY: Doubleday and Company, 1964).

Bruce, Robert V., *Lincoln and the Tools of War* (Urbana, IL: University of Illinois Press, 1989).

Duff, Scott A., *The M1 Garand: Post World War II* (Export, PA: Scott A. Duff, 1989).

Davis, William C., *The American Frontier* (Norman, OK: University of Oklahoma Press and Salamander Books, London, 1999).

Fjestad, S.P., *Blue Book of Gun Values*, 20th Edition (Minneapolis, MN: Blue Book Publications, 1999).

Flayderman, Norm, *Flayderman's Guide To Antique American Firearms and Their Values*, 7th Edition (Iola, WI: Krause Publications, 1998).

Houze, Herbert G., *Winchester Repeating Arms Company* (Iola, WI: Krause Publications, 1994).

Leckie, Robert, *The Wars of America* (New York, NY: Harper and Row, 1981).

Lott, Professor John R., *More Guns Less Crime* (Chicago: University of Chicago Press, 1998).

Madis, George, *The Winchester Book* (Brownsboro, TX: Art and Reference House, 1985).

McDowell, R. Bruce, *Evolution of the Winchester* (Tacoma, WA: Armory Publications, 1985).

McPherson, James M., *Battle Cry of Freedom* (New York: Oxford University Press, 1998).

Trolard, Tom, *Winchester Commemoratives* (Plano, TX: Commemorative Investments Press, 1985).

Wahl, Paul, and Toppel, Don, *The Gatling Gun* (New York, NY, Arco Publishing Company, 1971).

Williamson, Harold F., *Winchester: The Gun That Won The West* (Washington, D.C.: Combat Forces Press, 1952).

Wilson, R.L., *Winchester: An American Legend* (New York, NY, Random House, 1991).

INDEX

Winchester: *The Golden Age of American Gunmaking and the Winchester 1 of 1,000* (Cody, WY: Winchester Arms Museum, 1983).

The Book of Winchester Engraving (Los Angeles, CA, Beinfeld Publishing Co., 1976).

Winchester Engraving (Palm Springs, CA, Beinfeld Publishing Co., 1989).

The Peacemakers: Arms and Adventure in the American West (New York, NY, Random House, 1992).

Steel Canvas: The Art of American Arms (New York, NY, Random House, 1995).

PERIODICALS

American Rifleman, National Rifle Association, Fairfax, VA.
Guns & Ammo, Petersen Publishing Co., Los Angeles, CA.
Man At Arms*, Andrew Mowbray, Inc., Lincoln, RI.
The Gun Report*, Worldgun Report, Inc., Aledo, IL
The Winchester Collector, Winchester Arms Collectors Association, Brownsboro, TX.
* Includes listings of collectors'gun shows.

ARTICLES

Bailey, Harold L. Jr., "Some Examples of the Use of Firearms

in the Mining Industry Circa 1860-1980," *Journal of the American Society of Arms Collectors*, April 1996.
Ball, Gene, and Dow, Richard, "Winchester's New Museum Opens," *Man At Arms*, July/August,1980.
Canfield, Bruce N.:
"The Wartime Winchesters," *Man At Arms*, July/August, 1986.
"The Army's 'Light Rifle,'" *American Rifleman*, February 1996.
"Winchester Goes to War," *American Rifleman*, August, 1999.
Houze, Herbert G., "The Henry and Model 1866 Serial Numbering," *Man At Arms*, July/August, 1991.
Hunnicutt, Robert W., "The Return of the Rifleman's Rifle," *American Rifleman*, March, 1994.
Keefe, Mark A. IV, A Pair of Supreme Over-Unders," *American Rifleman*, July 2000
Richardson, H.L., "Going Under Down Under," *Guns & Ammo*, February 2000.
Rattenbury, Richard, "A Winchester for All Seasons," *Man At Arms*, September/October 1986.
Truslow, Henry A., "This Henry Tells a Story," *Journal of the American Society of Arms Collectors*, May 1999.
